Blue, Blue Sky

PAMELA GREGORY

APPRECIATION

I am so grateful to have the support of my friends and family not only in the writing of this book, but in life. Thank you, Heather for inspiration; Sandy and Donna for all your ideas and corrections; my sisters for your encouragement; and Jackie – thank you for loving Mama and being there for better and for worse.

DEDICATION

I am writing this for my daughter, Aja, because in our times together we talk less and less about the sad times, and for my family, so they will know what Mama went through and how brave she was. And for those struggling with dementia, to give them hope in this life and eternally. This is also for the caregivers. I hope this will give you courage to put on a smile and make the best of things. You *can* smile through the tears. Above all I write for the Lord of all, sweet Jesus. I pray this will bring glory and honor to Him.

TABLE OF CONTENTS

PREFACE

This is not an easy task. Going through it wasn't easy. Some of you may wonder why I would detail some of the worst days of my mother's life. I write this only to show her faith and her strength and to inspire and help others facing similar situations.

I could not describe the things we went through without first helping you to know my mother as she was before the decline. I hope you will fall in love with her too.

All is Well

Sixty-Two Years

SUNSHINE, BLUE, BLUE SKY
& GREEN GRASS

My earliest memory is of the blue, blue sky and gently sloping hills of green grass. The Missouri sun is not only brilliant, but you can feel it. The air is warm and alive with it.

I think I was at the driving range Daddy owned when I was three years old. I don't really remember the golfers, the metal baskets of balls, or the shop that I know was there. But wait. If I try, I think I can remember the shop. It was more of a shed. It was an empty-ish, drab, building with a cement floor. It's understandable that I would forget the gray details of the shop when there were such brilliant colors outside.

In life, if we are kind to ourselves, we allow our minds to drift away from the painful times that squeeze the color out of life. So before I drift too far, I will write about this very precious, but painful time in our lives, so I can begin to forget.

A SISTER

My mother was exceptional. She was beautiful, graceful, and strong. To this child growing up in the 1960s, my mommy was the car driver; she was the boss, so pretty, always clean, and stylish. As she drove, she sang. We sang along with The Fifth Dimension's, "Up, Up and Away" on the radio. We sang at home too. Daddy's parents, (we

3

called them Mom and Pop) gave us a wonderfully large, wooden, Curtis Mathes, tabletop radio and it sat in the dining room by the window. While she cleaned, we listened. The curtains fluttered in the gentle afternoon breeze as the Beatles sang, "I Want to Hold Your Hand". And then, "O' sweet pea, won't you dance with me, won't you, won't you, won't you dance with me." And she took my hands and danced with me across the shining hardwood floor.

I remember her being pregnant. I was only four. I don't think I really understood why her tummy was so big until she fell down the stairs in the middle of the night. The upstairs potty was out of order, so we were using the bathroom in the basement. One night Mama tumbled all the way down the stairs. It was so loud it woke me up and I heard her crying. I cautiously, made my way down the first few stairs. Daddy was with her. She was lying on a bed down there. I could barely see them.

"Mommy?" I whispered.

"She's okay, just a few bruises, but be careful if you're coming down, the stairs are wet," he said. "She wet her pants."

Well, she was on her way to the bathroom after all, I thought. "But she's crying," I said.

"But she's crying mostly because she's worried about the baby," Daddy explained.

That was the first time I realized something bad could actually happen to my mama. And I decided I would

4

always try to help her.

I tried to help her with my baby sister, but it seemed that no one could make Susan happy but Mama. Susan was beautiful and sweet, and a mommy's girl from the very start. Somehow, Susan attached herself to Mama and wouldn't let go. So I decided the best way to help would be to stay out of the way and mind Mama. I observed others trying to help. Mama's cousin, Darlene stayed with us one evening, and asked me if I knew how to make my sister stop crying. I didn't know how. She wanted Mama. No matter who was with us, Susan would cry until Mama came home.

When Susan got old enough to stand, she would hold onto Mama's leg while she was cooking or doing dishes. One day at the laundromat, I noticed Susan had attached herself to the leg of a strange woman. I quickly ran to the other side of the row of washers to get Mama. I pulled Mama by the hand, around to the other side. When Susan saw us coming around the corner, she looked up at the woman and melted into tears. I remember that look, "Oh, no! Then who are you?"

We always teased Susan about clinging, but throughout her life Susan has maintained that strong connection with our mother. While I pursued boys, college, and a better paying job, Susan nurtured her mothering instincts and became more like Mama. Always the talker, Susan kept the conversations going, actually listened to our mother's advice, and as far as I know never disappointed her.

COUNTRY LIVING

Mama grew up in a large family in a small town in the foothills of the Ozark Mountains in Western Arkansas. She was the ninth child in a family of ten. They had a modest house on six acres. My grandparents kept things simple and through the years their home didn't change too much. It was just a four room cottage with a living room and kitchen on one side and two bedrooms on the other. On the front of the house, there were four windows and two doors. I always wondered why there were two doors. There was a much loved porch swing with gray peeling paint on the long, wooden porch that ran the length of the house. The house faced north and little violets grew in the shade around the front step.

When Mama was growing up, they drew their water from a well. If you wanted hot water it had to be heated on the stove. Grandma made lye soap and used it to wash their clothes under a sycamore tree in the backyard. In the early days, she used a wash tub and scrub board. Later, she had a washer with a hand cranked wringer. In the kitchen, there was always a bucket of water with an aluminum dipper on the wash stand. I don't think I drank enough water as a child, but when I was at Grandpa and Grandma's house, I couldn't get enough. The water was so cool and tasted so clean. I would drink my fill, which would ultimately result in a trip past the garden to the outhouse.

As you stepped into the dim light of the wooden outhouse you could see there were two holes to choose from, one with a padded seat that Grandma used and one for the men to use. As you pulled the door closed, you turned a block of wood that was nailed to it so it wouldn't swing open. Slivers of light beamed through the cracks in the door revealing a roll of paper that hung on a loop of wire. You might notice flies buzzing somewhere behind you or a granddaddy longlegs feeling his way up the wall. It was nothing fancy, but it worked.

Grandma kept chickens and a milk cow. As a child, I remember seeing her milk the cow. She would go out early in the morning and again in the evening, with a stool in one hand and a bucket in the other. She showed me how and let me try it once, but she was pretty much all business. She made butter in a churn on the front porch and kept it in the bucket down in the well to keep it cool.

Once I watched her wring a chicken's neck. There was no hesitation. She calmly reached down and grabbed the chicken by the neck and swung it around. She knew the motion by heart and had no intention of getting pecked or scratched. Then when she let go of the crazy chicken it ran around the yard with its head dangling. Life isn't always pretty.

Grandma grew strawberries in front of the chicken pen. She would weed and hoe the little mounds in the early summer sun, tending them until they yielded sweet, red berries which she turned into wonderful strawberry preserves. She also had an apple tree which she guarded from blackbirds and tree climbing grandkids. Every year she would store her labors behind a curtain in the "fruit closet" in the bedroom.

Now that I have my own garden, I think of what I could have learned had I been a more practical child and helped Grandma and Grandpa more.   Instead, I was the observer, perched in a tree by the front porch while Grandma churned the butter or the explorer finding toads between the corn stalks.   Grandma would calmly say, "Don't hurt my toads; they're good for the garden. They eat the bugs."

Grandma was well known in town for giving hair cuts. Many afternoons, a young boy or two would come by to see if she had time to give them a hair cut. She would sit them on a stool on the front porch or in the middle of the living room and in nothin' flat the clippers had done their work and she had another quarter in her pocket.

On Sunday's Grandma would put on her Sunday dress and walk to the little Assembly of God church around the corner. She watched the TV evangelists: Jimmy Swaggart, Oral Roberts, and my favorite, Billy Graham. I remember passing through the living room seeing Grandma with her Bible open in her lap.

Grandpa didn't go to church with Grandma that I can remember, but I heard that when he was younger he loved to sing. Mama told me he led singing in the church when she was young and was part of a gospel singing group that was featured on local radio at times. And I have seen a faded, paperback hymnal with Grandpa's name handwritten in the front cover.

When I think of Grandpa, I see him in the morning sipping his coffee from a saucer where he poured it to cool. He showed me how to mix butter and honey for my biscuit. I also think of Hi Ho Crackers. He would come in and grab a handful of crackers and go back outside. Inside was Grandma's domain. Outside was where the men worked and smoked. He kept a pouch of tobacco in his pocket and when it was time to gab, he would get out his rolling paper and roll up a cigarette.

Grandpa kept coon dogs, and a mule, which he used to plow the garden. In the spring, he could be seen walking his mule down the road headed to plow a neighbor's garden. He grew all the usual vegetables and peanuts, which he kept in a barrel in the old smokehouse. That's where he kept all the tools and Grandma's empty jars. By the time I was old enough to investigate the smokehouse many of the tools had been retired and hung from the ceiling collecting cobwebs and dust and rust. There was also a set of National Geographic magazines in the smokehouse, which I looked at often.

The smokehouse had one more amenity I must mention. On the back side of the smokehouse, was Grandpa's shower. He had mounted a barrel on a stand up near the roof. It had a plug in it and it was open at the top to collect rain water. In the summer he would put well water in it and by the end of the day, it would be warm. Below the barrel he built a screen of wood on two sides for privacy. After a long, hot day, Grandpa could enjoy a shower.

That reminds me, when my mother got sick and I began to spend more time with her, one of the first things I had to help her with was adjusting the water for her shower.

I remember one summer day, when I was little, Mama

drawing water and heating it on the stove for a bath for my sister Susan and me. We set a big galvanized washtub between the well and the kitchen door and waited until the sun started to go down so the neighbors couldn't see. Then she filled the tub up about half way with cold water from the well and added enough hot water from the stove to heat the water. I was dusty from running around barefoot all day so she bathed Susan first. Then it was my turn. I was old enough to bathe myself. It was such a wonderful, simple pleasure - to be clean, outside at dusk.

Around the Fourth of July, there would be quite a gathering. Uncles, aunts, and cousins came to visit family they hadn't seen all year. There would be sweet iced tea, fried chicken, corn on the cob, green beans, fried okra and squash, biscuits and watermelon. Sometimes, if we were lucky, there was homemade ice cream. The kids would occupy themselves with fireworks, locust shells, swimming, and lightning bugs.

Some time during all of this celebrating, Grandpa would take us for a ride in the back of his faded old blue-green Chevy to the little family owned grocery store on Main Street. There wasn't much on Main Street besides the store, just a couple of churches and a tiny post office. As we climbed into the hot bed of the truck, he would roll his toothpick out of the way and ask, "Don't you have some shoes you can put on?"

And he would hand out quarters for us to spend at the store. "Alright now, hold on and don't sit on the edge. Sit down on the hump or on the bed."

And off we'd go, barefoot, in our cutoff jean shorts and

tank tops, wind in our hair, suntanned faces peering around the cab of the truck. Then one of the older kids would ease up to sit on the edge, careful to be seen holding firmly. And one or two brave ones would follow suite to sit dangerously on the sides of the bed. Grandpa would drive oh so slowly over the railroad tracks and around the corners through town.

As we filed past the old men in overalls on the bench outside the store I overheard bits of conversation. "Those are Tom's grandkids." And Grandpa visited with the men outside while we happily spent our quarters. Twenty-five cents would buy a bottle of soda and a sack full of candy carefully selected, piece by piece, through the glass of the candy case. If you didn't know the name of the candy or if you were soft spoken or if you were just too little, you could point at the candy you wanted and one of the store owners, Frankie or Virginia, would try to figure out which kind you wanted.

"Is this the one you want? Candy cigarettes? Chick-O-Stick? " They patiently asked.

Grandma enjoyed sewing. Her old machine wasn't electric. It had a treadle she worked with her feet. She made most of her own dresses and her cotton slips. Often she would "take up" clothing to make it fit. As long as I can remember, Grandma had a little pouch made of white cloth where she kept her money. She kept it pinned with a safety pin inside the top of her slip. If you were going to the store for her, she would reach in and unpin it, take out the money to give to you and pin it right back. The fact that she kept her money near to her heart didn't mean it was dear to her heart. She did guard it though and she saved it like no one else I've ever known. And Grandma didn't let anything to go to waste. Waste not, want not. She was a natural recycler. Much of the fabric she used was given to her. When I was pregnant with my son, Austin, she made some washcloths out of soft flannel for me to use on his soft bottom. She crocheted around the edges. She knew how to "make do" and even whittled her own crochet needles.

Like most quilters of previous generations, she often used material from old clothes to make quilts. Her quilting frame hung neatly near the living room ceiling. In the old days, she made many practical quilts from flour sack cloth. The quilt tops and bottoms were pieced together from large rectangular blocks of fabric cut from the flour sacks. Then a thin layer of cotton was laid between. The quilting on these simple, but colorful quilts was in straight lines an inch and a half apart running the length of the quilt. With ten kids I'm sure more than a few quilts were made and used up.

I remember spending the night in Grandma's bed. We would come to visit in the summer when school was out and would stay for a couple of weeks. Mama always slept with Susan in the spare bed and I slept with Grandma. Her bed was up against the window to the front porch and at night the choir of frogs and crickets filled the night as cool, moist air drifted in. You were always warm in Grandma's bed tucked under the heavy layer of quilts.

As she got older, and had more time, Grandma and her friends from the church made many beautiful quilts.

Mama found time to work with her on a few. She was proud of the quilts she made with her mother.

Mama inherited Grandma's ability with the needle and thread. She was happiest when she had the sewing machine humming. When I was young, we took trips to the fabric store where we enjoyed looking at the giant pattern books. Sometimes Mama would let me pick out a pattern. Then we would choose the material. I would rub the fabric between my fingers just like she did. That's just how you look at fabric. Then at home it would be patterns crinkling, and the sound of the scissors against the tabletop. And soon she would call, "Come in here, so I can measure you."

Then she would say, "Stand up straight. Hold your arms out a little, away from your sides."

Something about her measuring, the way she held the tape around my waist, fussing to get the straight pins in place, and the length just right, made me feel so cared for. Even in high school, I loved the cotton dresses she made for me.

She took pride in her clothes, and took care to always be neat, clean, ironed, and mended. It showed in her embrace long after she could no longer sew. If you stayed in her arms long enough, she would straighten your shirttail or pull your shirt sleeve down.

Mama had a knack for making something out of nothing. She didn't spend a lot of money decorating, yet when she finished it looked like something out of Better Homes & Gardens. Once Mama's niece, Dorsie, commented that, "No matter where Aunt Glenda ends up, she always makes her home look like a little doll house." Mama grew up in a home where most of their possessions were necessary for survival. When I think about Grandma's house it isn't Better Homes & Gardens that comes to mind. It was more like somewhere between Country Living and National Geographic. Okay, it wasn't *that* bad. They had enough, but not much extra. They were comfortable. Besides her quilts, and a picture of Jesus, the lilac bush in the backyard may have been the most beautiful thing Grandma owned.

As Mama went forward with her own life, I think she appreciated and enjoyed the blessings of modern life…

A NEW START

When Daddy and Mama got married, Mama was accepted by her new in-laws unconditionally. Daddy's parents, Mom and Pop, didn't care that she had been married before or that she brought with her a nine-month old baby girl. They wrapped us up into their lives and never looked back. I became their first grandchild.

Mom treated Mama like a daughter. She introduced to her a new way of living. They spent time shopping together and preparing meals for the family. On holidays, they would set the table with their finest cloth napkins, their best linen tablecloth, and an elegant centerpiece, taking care to lay out the silverware in the proper places.

Mom prepared many wonderful meals in her "roaster oven." It was a stand-alone slow cooker with a rotisserie attachment on a rolling cabinet. In it she made the most savory arm roasts with carrots, celery, onions, and potatoes. Daddy and Uncle Butch would always liven up the meals with stories and jokes. Daddy would tease, "When Mom cooks we pray AFTER we eat."

On Thanksgiving, she would rotisserie a turkey, but on Christmas she would glaze a ham with mustard and brown sugar and cover it with pineapple slices and cherries held in place with toothpicks. Add to that, mashed potatoes and green beans simmered with bacon drippings and onions - and homemade rolls, and pie. Mama adopted those recipes and traditions and made them her own.

SUMMER VISITS AT MOM & POP'S

I was only seven when we moved to Oklahoma. With the distance came new traditions, like holiday cards and letters. At Christmas, boxes of gifts came in the mail with tags that read, "Love Always, Mom & Pop." And there were summertime visits. Every year, Susan and I would spend time in Missouri with Mom and Pop.

Pop was the golf pro at the country club. Mom minded the pro shop while he gave lessons. She took as much time off as she could while we were there, but sometimes she had to work. While Mom worked, Susan stayed with Uncle Butch and Aunt Helen and their boys. Since I was a little older, I went to work with Mom and spent my day in the pool at the golf course. At lunch Mom took me to the club house for a club sandwich and a cherry 7Up. If he wasn't too busy, Pop would give me a golf lesson. On the way to the driving range, our golf cart would whiz through the cool air under the tall pine trees. As we passed by the golfers gathered on the greens, he would slow down and we would quietly watch while someone made a putt.

In the evenings, Mom would let us help with dinner. We would often bake chicken covered with Rice Krispies. She would get out the rolling pin and crunch up Rice Krispies under wax paper. I would dip the pieces of chicken in evaporated milk and roll them in the Rice Krispies. She taught me how to make the best cole slaw. I always enjoyed turning the grater to grind the cabbage and carrots. And it was always a treat for Susan and me to help cut out sugar cookies.

Pop thought it was important for us girls to have a little spending money while we were visiting. And he had a unique way of getting it to us. At dinner, he would wait until our plates were almost clean and then he would say, "You forgot to look under your plate." So Susan and I would peek under our plates and there would be two or three dollars, or a five dollar bill! Then we'd jump up and give Pop a big thank you hug and a kiss.

After dinner, we would help dry the dishes with Mom's hand embroidered tea towels. While we worked, she would sing along with Nat King Cole and try to get me to impersonate Louis Armstrong singing Hello Dolly. And she would happily hum along with The Lennon Sisters on Laurence Welk. But I think her favorite was Andy Williams' Moon River. Mom has been gone a long time now, but every time I hear Moon River, I cry. I miss those days.

When it got close to bedtime, Pop would ask, "Do you

want to have a bowl of cereal with me before you go to bed?"

I remember having Kellogg's Cornflakes, Rice Krispies, Shredded Wheat, and sometimes Frosted Flakes. Pop and I always used half and half on our cereal at bedtime and we never left the milk in the bottom of the bowl. Pop would say, "Bottoms up!" And we would raise our bowls and finish it off.

Then Mom would come to take us off to bed with clippies and scotch tape on her hair to hold the curls in place around her face. She would take us to tinkle and then tuck us into twin beds with a kiss, reminding us to say our prayers. When they lived out in the country, our bedroom was upstairs and she didn't want us to fall down the stairs in the dark, so she showed us the little ceramic chamber pot sitting by the wall, "If you have to go in the middle of the night, use this."

I knew how cold that would be. I nodded my head, but I remember thinking, *No thanks. I'll hold it.*

Sometimes when I look back, I long for those times when we were all young and strong and the world seemed safe. Back then, somewhere in my mind the town crier rang, "All is well!"

And the world was as it should be.

While we were there, Mom usually found the time to take us to the museum to look at the egg collection and the beaded Indian leather. As we drove through the city streets, Mom would remind us to lock our doors. You never know when someone desperate might try to get in the car at a stop light. On Fridays, Mom would take us downtown to the beauty shop. We waited while she had her hair done and then she would take us shopping. We always went home from Mom and Pop's with plenty of school clothes.

While we were running errands, we would often stop for a hamburger at a restaurant where the tables had little jukeboxes on them. Sometimes, on the way home, we would stop at the fruit market where she would buy a little basket of peaches so we could have sliced peaches, with half and half, sprinkled with sugar for breakfast.

At the grocery store, Mom would make conversation with the people in line. She would talk about the weather, the prices, and her ailments. When she was a teenager, she had rheumatic fever, which damaged her heart. And she had arthritis. Her knuckles were swollen and painful. Daddy and Uncle Butch always teased her about telling everyone her life history. Dad said, "Mom, when you die, I'm going to have them put, 'I told you I was sick' on your headstone." I didn't think it was very funny. Between Daddy and Uncle Butch, it was a joke a minute. At times you didn't know if they were joking or telling the truth.

On Sunday mornings we went to church at the Methodist church. The floors creaked and the hymns echoed in the old church where Uncle Butch and Aunt Helen were so involved. After church we went out for lunch. As I slid our trays along, with the silverware and iced tea, I politely answered Mom's questions about roast beef and gravy, all the time eyeing the fresh strawberry pie at the end of the glass case. Then we would go to visit Pop's mother, Grandmother Garrison.

Grandmother Garrison was so sweet. Her wrinkled face felt so soft as you kissed her powdered cheek. She always fussed over us girls in her southern Mississippi accent, "Oh my goodness, look how much you girls have grown. I wouldn't have recognized you." And she would rattle on about her worries and her TV soaps as I tried out all her chairs. "Would you like me to fix you something to eat?" she asked.

"No, Mother, we just had lunch," Pop would say. So she continued with the latest news about Pop's brothers and sisters and their families. And she told us about an angel that spoke to her at her bedside once.

No matter where we went they would run into people they knew. Mom used to tell a story about taking me to visit one of her dear friends when I was only four years old. The nice lady showed me her piano and asked me if I knew a song to sing. I was reluctant to sing and told her, "When I get a big mouth like you, I will sing too." After hearing that story a few times, I was always careful to watch my words when meeting new people.

They were such encouragers. They would introduce us and tell everyone how proud they were of their grandchildren. They always found something to brag about, how helpful we were or what good grades we made. They always told me to study hard in school and make good grades. They said, "Go to college and get an education. You can be anything you want to be."

Mom and Pop did what they could to make us feel good about ourselves. They showed their love by being involved in our lives. And it took an effort being so far away.

OKLAHOMA

In his younger days, Daddy had gone to college. Then he was in the Air National Guard. Susan was born in 1965, and a year later he got out of the Guard. Soon after, an opportunity to work as assistant golf pro drew us to Oklahoma. I remember Christmas that year. Mama woke us up early to see what Santa brought. Daddy and his friend from the golf club had stayed up all night putting together a cardboard mini-kitchen. There was a refrigerator, a stove, and cabinets with plastic dishes and a bowl of real fruit and nuts on the counter. They were all pink trimmed in black. Susan and I stood blinking in the early morning light. We couldn't believe our eyes.

It wasn't long before Daddy decided to go into business. I can't remember all the companies he started, or was a partner in. He had an entrepreneurial passion and was determined to succeed. Of course, he would always succeed at golf. He has always been a member of the PGA. As long as I can remember, he has travelled to tournaments and given lessons. One day he golfed with Bob Hope who was in town for a park dedication. He brought home an autograph for me. But golfing wasn't all he wanted to do.

So while I played hopscotch and practiced cartwheels in

the backyard, he sold vitamins and started a men's custom suit business that took him to Hong Kong and back. While he was building an auto club multi-level business, I was making mud pies and catching horned toads. While he was smoking cigars on business trips, I was cooking in my Easy Bake Oven and dressing Barbies in clothes Mama made on her sewing machine.

My dad has always been loaded with ambition, but in between all the business, we found time for ice cream, eating out, and fishing at the lake. One day he came home carrying what looked like a briefcase, but it turned out to be a record player, for me. At that time, I was in love with the Partridge Family and David Cassidy. Daddy took me to my first concert. We stood among the screaming girls and watched as David Cassidy sang "I Think I Love You" in his white fringed jumpsuit.

I used to ride my bike to school, to Sherri and Terri's house (they were my best friends), and to my piano lessons. On September 3rd, when I was eleven, I was on my way home from a piano lesson when I was hit by a car. It was so hot, and I was trying to decide whether to go straight and get an Icee at the 7-Eleven or turn right and get home. I made a mistake. It was a blind corner with a retaining wall and shrubbery partially blocking my view and I didn't see the car. I had decided to skip the Icee, problem was, I skipped the stop sign. By the time I saw the car, I was already out too far to get out of the way. My piano lesson books went flying and the bike rolled to a stop by the curb. I flew over the top of the car and landed behind it. The driver was a very nice lady who was visibly upset and concerned. Her son was picking up my things for me. But my leg was broken. Thank goodness that was all.

I spent five weeks in the hospital in traction hanging by my knees and six weeks in a body cast at home. It was so hard on everyone. I had to rely on someone else to do everything for me. Mama's youngest brother, Uncle Kenny, was in Vietnam. So his wife at that time, Aunt Bev, came to stay with us and helped take care of me so Mama could work.

On Halloween, Mama cut up an old white sheet and wrapped me up like a mummy. I was still in the body cast, so she only had to wrap the top half. Then she put a twin mattress out on the porch and they carried me out there. Since the accident, the trip home from the hospital was the only time I had been outside. I had been cooped up for two months. It was great to be in the fresh air! We even had scary music playing in the window. I handed out candy to the kids that were brave enough to approach.

Two years later, when I was thirteen, Mama and Daddy divorced. It was hard for me to understand why. But I could accept it. Daddy came to me and told me how it would be and that he loved me and that he would be alright. It was the noblest and the best thing he could have done for me. The problems between them did not change the way I felt about either of them. I knew I loved them both.

I don't remember asking why they divorced, but when we got back to Arkansas, I did overhear Mama tell Grandma something about how silly it was to have a phone in the car, but never know if there was going to be enough money for groceries at the end of the week. Maybe there was more to it than that. I don't know. But I do know we were never hungry. It doesn't matter now. They did the best they could and it just didn't work out. Isn't that the way it usually is?

I reserved a place for him in my heart, but I knew about distance and that sometimes you had to wait a long time to see someone you love. That didn't mean you stopped loving them. Just because you didn't see them every day didn't mean they weren't thinking of you.

A NEW JOB, A NEW FAMILY, AND A NEW HOME

We stayed with Grandma and Grandpa while Mama got on her feet. At first, she took a job working as a waitress at night, and then found a job in a factory that paid a little better. It wasn't long before she found something she really liked. Ace Hardware opened a store about 25 miles away and they hired a great group of people that worked together as friends, but felt like family. Mama adopted the housewares department and settled in. At work, she applied the same standards and energy she used at home to make our lives better. She believed in giving her employer an honest day's work. She knew if she were paying someone to work for her, she would expect them to be doing their job, so she did hers. She said, "If it's worth doing, do it well." She worked there until they closed the doors twenty years later.

It wasn't too long after we moved to Arkansas that

Mama's cousin, Darlene talked Mama into a blind date. Darlene's husband had a friend who was recently divorced.

"I wish you would find Jackie a date," he told Darlene.

"You're right. I think Glenda would be good for Jackie. I'll see what I can do," she said.

After a few months of dating, Jackie made up his mind that she was the one. He bought an album by Hank Williams Jr. and brought it to her. As it played on my record player, he went back outside to the car and returned with eleven yellow roses.

A few months later, Mama was down with the flu and Jackie was doing all he could to take care of her. He cooked meals for Susan and me and ran the errands while she was sick. One evening when it was time for him to go, neither of them wanted him to leave. Mama told him, "Jackie, if you're going to be here all the time why don't we get married."

They began their life together. They would help each other through the next 38 years. It turned out to be a really good thing.

Jackie had two daughters and a son. We met Marty right away, since she lived near us. She was the youngest, only three years old when Mama and Jackie married. They brought her to our home on Wednesdays and every other weekend. We immediately fell in love with her. She was a little angel. Her hair was so light it was almost white and it was so easy to make her smile. She loved to sing and always dressed so pretty. She was well behaved and she loved her daddy. She would love Mama too.

I have found that loving a new parent doesn't mean you love the others any less. Just like a mother who has a new baby to love doesn't love the other children any less. Sometimes it is a challenge to divide your time, but that's always a challenge.

We had to wait a little longer to meet Jackie's older children, Jacqueline Kay and Steven. But soon we made the four hour drive to bring them home for a visit. Jack (she didn't like her long name) was only a year younger than me. I was 13. I liked the idea of having a new brother and a sister that was close to my age. I hoped we would be good friends. And we were.

We started having fun right away. On the ride home we were traveling behind a Frito Lay delivery truck and it made us crave chips. So we devised a plan, "I wonder, if we make a sign, if the delivery man will give us some chips." So we found paper and pen and went to work quickly. Our sign read, in big block letters, "LAYS POTATO CHIPS, PLEASE!"

So when we passed the truck, he looked over to see our sign and our begging faces scrunched up to the window in the back seat. He either felt sorry for us trapped in the back seat or he thought we were funny, because he waved us down. Jackie and Mama were surprised and not quite sure what was going on, but we were excited and giggling, because the nice delivery man had two bags of chips tucked under his arm. "Would your kids like some chips?" he asked with a smile.

After Mama and Jackie had been married a year or so, they bought a little three bedroom house around the corner from Grandma and Grandpa's. It wasn't much to look at, but it had potential, and the price was right.

As long as I can remember, Mama had an endless energy for homemaking that was beyond the rest of us. And she dragged us into her plans at every opportunity. If she was working we needed to be working. I remember my new sister, Jack, getting to know Mama's tidy ways. Before we could move the furniture into the living room and kitchen, Mama insisted we scrub the floor. She gave each of us a toothbrush and showed us the little grooves in the vinyl that were not supposed to be brown. Down on our hands and knees, Jack looked at the yellow floor and then looked up at me and said, "But they're supposed to be brown aren't they?" I just smiled.

Mama had a vision of life and how it should be, and it included us. If we got home before she did in the evening, it was our job to have something laid out to thaw and the kitchen ready for her to start dinner when she got home. We all helped with the cooking from time to time. Well, maybe all but Marty. I guess she was too little. But she remembers Mama teaching her to set the table. Everyone got to help.

At dinner we were expected to sit at the table and have conversation. If the TV was on, and becoming a distraction, she would ask one of us to turn it off. And as needed, she would remind us of our manners.

"There are certain subjects that aren't appropriate to discuss at the table."

26

"Chew with your mouth closed."

"Don't take such big bites."

"Slow down and chew your food."

"Use your napkin."

"Use your fork, not your fingers."

"Don't play with your food."

"Don't reach across the table. Pass the potatoes please."

And the one I heard the most, "Sit up straight."

I tried putting my foot in the chair once or twice with my knee sticking up above the edge of the table. "Get your foot out of the chair, Uncle Ward," she said. Uncle Ward was Mama's uncle, but she obviously didn't approve of his table manners.

And after dinner, we would argue about whose turn it was to wash the dishes and who would get to rinse. I was pretty good at getting out of washing. I always had to go to the bathroom after I ate dinner, but they never believed me. They accused me of hiding with the Reader's Digest while they did the dishes.

Not long after moving in, Mama tackled the job of redecorating the kitchen. She refinished the kitchen cabinets and replaced the hardware. She didn't just paint the cabinets; she antiqued them using a process that required multiple coats, and she didn't just replace the knobs, but the hinges too. Then on the wall above the counters, she installed a vinyl wall covering that looked and felt like bricks. To complete the project she mounted walnut stained shutters on the windows. She stained them herself, of course.

Soon she added a beautiful new door that had a window with beveled leaded glass that sent rainbows across the kitchen and living room in the evenings. She always loved that door. Even after they moved away, she would often find it convenient to drive past the little yellow house to gaze at that door.

The outside improvements included an awning, yellow siding, and a clear storm door. They moved a small building into the backyard to become Jackie's upholstering shop. It was also used to shelter the mower, the garden tools and boxes of things that couldn't be thrown away.

Then the planting began. They made a garden that produced fresh tomatoes, squash, cucumbers, and okra. In the yard, there were banana trees and elephant ears, forsythia, rose of Sharon, bright red poppies, and roses wreathed with sedum. A green, green lawn completed the picture. It was a little piece of heaven.

Every Saturday morning we would clean. My sister, Jack, says, "We didn't have spring cleaning, we had Saturday cleaning." One day Jack tried to get out of cleaning, "Do we really have to do this today?" Then she recalls Mama huffing into our room with a tote bag, acting like she was mad, pulling a couple of shirts out of the closet, stuffing them in the tote bag and handing it to her. Mama said, "The Whiner Train stops here in just a few minutes. You can get on it and take it as far as you want, but when you decide to come back, all the cleaning will still be here waiting." Jack was saying, "No way," as Mama proceeded to push her out into the hall. About that time, Jackie walked past and muttered something about living in a house of crazies.

If it was racing season, Saturday nights would find us at the stock car races where Jackie knew everyone. He worked in the pits and we always got there early and stayed until almost everyone had gone. Sometimes I sold programs at the front gate and a few times I appeared in the program as trophy girl, presenting a trophy to the winner of last week's big race. It was a big honor to be the trophy girl, and a little scary, but all the winners were gentlemen and limited the kissing to a peck on the cheek.

On Sundays we would visit Jackie's folks. He had three sisters and seven brothers and sometimes I think they all showed up at once. If the weather was cold or wet, the house would be packed. You had to turn sideways to get through the narrow spots. The rooms were full of laughter and teasing. The tantalizing smell of fried chicken and freshly baked bread surrounded us as the men told their hunting stories and bragged on trades they'd made. There were always uncles picking on kids, sisters telling on brothers, and moms getting onto everyone. And there was plenty to eat. It's not the size of the house that makes you feel welcome in a home, but the size of the heart.

Things weren't always calm and quiet around our house either. My mother had a way of letting you know if you had crossed the line and if you persisted, you could get an earful of righteous anger. She did her best to keep us all in line. When I would start down the wrong path she would reel me in. She'd say, "You're not going out of this house with those shorts on. And don't give me any guff." That meant, don't talk back. And when I brought home music that was undeniably raunchy, she said, "Not under my roof," and she burned my records.

She also didn't let us say the F word, and I'm not talking about the one you think I'm talking about. The F word she wouldn't let us say had to do with passing gas, which meant we had to excuse ourselves and go outside or to the bathroom.

And the kids weren't the only ones who had to tow the line. For the first couple of years after Mama and Jackie married, he still drank more beer than Mama wanted him to. One day she let him know she wasn't going to put up with it and threw her coffee cup at the door of the little upholstery shop leaving a permanent reminder. She wasn't afraid to fight for her peace of mind.

A few years later, during their weekly Uno game, Jackie's sister-in-law Phyllis wondered out loud, "I don't know how you stayed with him through all of that…"

Mama replied with a smile, "He was worth waiting on."

We almost had another sibling. I wonder if he was a boy or a girl. I don't remember if Mama knew she was pregnant or if the miscarriage was a complete surprise. I just remember Jackie waking me up in the middle of the night to tell me he was taking her to the hospital. As he carried her to the car he told me, "Try to clean up the mess if you can. I'll call you as soon as I can - as soon I know something." Her beautiful legs were the last thing I saw as he put her in the back seat. I cried and prayed as I cleaned up the blood. We almost lost her that night.

A MATTER OF THE HEART

When I was a little girl, Mama taught me to pray. We knelt beside my bed at night and prayed.

> Now I lay me down to sleep
> I pray the Lord my soul to keep.
> Thy love stay with me through the night
> Until the morning brings its light.
>   Amen

And then we would pray for our family. "God bless Mommy and Daddy, and Grandpa and Grandma and Mom and Pop, and Susan, and keep them safe. Amen."

We didn't attend church regularly while I was growing up, but always had a respect for God. I remember Mama teaching me the hymn, "Bringing in the Sheaves". She was singing as she sewed.

> Sowing in the morning,
> Sowing seeds of kindness,
> Sowing in the noontide
> And the dewy eves,
>
> Waiting for the harvest
> And the time of reaping,
> We shall come rejoicing
> Bringing in the sheaves.

31

> Bringing in the sheaves,
> Bringing in the sheaves,
> We shall come rejoicing
> Bringing in the sheaves.

I asked her, "Mommy, what is a sheave?"

I gave my heart to the Lord, as a teenager. I was invited to a youth group at the Methodist church. They met in an old house next door to the church. After some discussion about the Bible, we took turns praying for each other. They placed a chair, called the "prayer chair," in the center of the room and invited anyone needing prayer to sit in it. One by one people took their turn sitting in the chair. Some would ask us to pray for something specific and some would say, "I just need prayer." I knew I was having problems adjusting to life as a teenager in this new place; I was doing things I shouldn't, things I didn't even want to do. So when there was hesitation about who would sit in the chair next, I indicated I would like to be prayed for. I didn't say what for. I just sat in the chair and they laid their hands on my head and my shoulders.

They began to pray out loud. As I heard their words of faith spoken for me I felt love and compassion. I felt the presence of the Lord. The Holy Spirit was drawing me. After they prayed, the youth leader, Brother Jerry, asked me if I wanted to be saved, if I wanted to give my heart to Jesus. I said yes.

We walked over to the sanctuary and knelt at the altar. He explained to me how Jesus died to pay the price for our sins and that if we confess our sins He is faithful and just to forgive us our sins and cleanse us from all unrighteousness. All we have to do is ask.

I bowed my head and prayed that God would forgive my sins, cleanse my heart, and accept me as His child. I was thankful that God made a way for me to come to him. I made a commitment to learn more. I became a Christian and was baptized. I fell in love with Jesus and I fell in love with my Bible. I began to memorize scripture and seek the Lord in prayer.

I read a book called, Prison to Praise, by Merlin Carothers. In it, he shared how he learned to be thankful in every situation. He explained that all things work together for good for those who love God. I learned to praise God in every circumstance and that the joy of the Lord is my strength.

Soon I started going to church closer to home at the Assembly of God Church where my grandma went. I was looking for power. I needed strength. I wanted to be obedient. I wanted all that God had for me. I was surrounded by loving friends as I cried my heart out over and over at the altar praying for strength, wanting to please Him, asking God to cleanse me and use me, and praying for my family. As I poured my heart out, God poured His Spirit out. Joy and peace flooded my soul.

GROWING UP

The little yellow house with the banana trees and roses is where we lived during my high school years.

… It's where I dressed for homecoming.

… It's where Jack and I shared a room.

… It's where we got snowed in and worked puzzles.

… It's where I studied my Bible with newfound passion.

… It's where Marty sang Delta Dawn.

… It's where we ate watermelon.

… It's where Susan got braces.

… It's where we stayed up to watch the Midnight Special.

… It's where I addressed invitations to my wedding.

Jackie made friends with all the neighbors. Mr. Weese lived across the lane. He always had a nice garden. He told Jackie, "I've got tomatoes on an old door sitting on sawhorses over there. Now, I'm not going to bring you any, but if you ever run short on tomatoes just come on over and get what you need."

So one Sunday, while they were walking home from church, Marty overheard her dad say to Mama, "I'm gonna go steal some tomatoes from the Weese's for dinner." And off he went, across the lane and came back with a couple of fine, ripe tomatoes to slice with dinner.

Well, next Sunday at church, they asked if anyone needed prayer and little Marty piped up, "My daddy stole some of Mr. Weese's tomatoes this week. And it was on the way home from church!" Oops.

After I moved away from home, Steve and then Marty took their turns living with Mama and Jackie. When Steve was there, his dad would let him borrow the truck on the weekends. Finally, Mama told Steve, "If you're old enough to drive, you're old enough to get a job." So Steve would take the truck and go look for a job every chance he got, but the job search was taking way too long and in the meantime, he was running all the gas out of the truck.

One day, Mama decided to take matters into her own hands. "Steve, why don't you get dressed and I'll take you to apply for a job." To his dismay, she drove him to the chicken plant to apply for a job. They hired him right away. It was a job, but not the one he wanted. And that was back when gas was cheap!

… A few years later, it was where we brought our babies to see their Nanny and Papa. (That's what the kids called Mama and Jackie.)

Mama and Jackie loved to spend time with their grandchildren. They were always so proud of them. When my kids were little, they would ride with Papa around the yard on the mower (blades disengaged) until they were tired.

One day, when my son Austin was about two, he wandered around to the back of Nanny and Pa's house and then came running, all excited, to tell Papa, "Black diddos! Black diddos!" So they went to look and a swarm of mosquitoes had gathered over a puddle in the shade behind the house. We always laughed at the silly things the kids did and said. We all have our memories of those days to cherish.

… It was where Mama brought Grandma to try to take care of her after all of us were grown.

Grandma was in her eighties when her mind got to the point that she couldn't take care of herself. She couldn't stay at home alone, but she didn't want to stay at Mama's. She would say, "I've got to get home. Tom and the boys are there by themselves and I've got to go cook something for them to eat."

But there was no one there in the old house around the corner. Grandpa had been gone for a long time. She had gone back in time, maybe to a safer place, in her mind. Grandma walked out the door barefoot one day. Mama caught her as she started down the lane and led her through the snow back to the porch. After that, Mama found herself sleeping in the hall on the floor with her pillow so she could stop Grandma from leaving the house if she got up in the middle of the night. It was just too much to handle, so they had to move Grandma to a nursing home.

LONG DISTANCE RELATIONSHIPS

I didn't get to spend time in Missouri with Mom and Pop after I left home. Mom had to have open heart surgery the year after I was married. It was so hard to be far away and to know that I would be losing her. But she got well and her letters kept on coming, filled with recipes, and coupons, and encouraging words.

Daddy got married again. He was in Oklahoma City, when he met Sharon, and discovered she was from his home town. As they talked they realized their paths had crossed before. When Daddy was just out of high school, his golfing buddy was dating her. And in a previous relationship, Dad would drop the kids off at the babysitter's house on the way to work. The sitter's mother would often wave as he drove away. That was Sharon too. It was meant to be.

When my kids were old enough to go to school, I went back to college. By then Pop's ashes were scattered on one of the greens at the country club. He had finished his course. Mom was getting very fragile, but when I had completed my second year of college, she came to visit and told me, "Pop would be so proud of you." By the time I graduated from college, receiving my bachelor's degree Mom was gone too.

I remember when Uncle Butch and Aunt Helen, moved a small mobile home, out to the lake and parked it next door to them so they could take care of her. Then when she was in the hospital, Uncle Butch would stop by every morning on his way to work and feed her. I wished I could have been there, but I had to work and take care of my children. I wanted to help, but I couldn't be there. It just isn't right to be so far away from someone you love when they are hurting.

In some ways, you might say there was a distance between my mother and me. We didn't always agree. She tried to guide me. She tried to give me advice, but I didn't have the strength to follow. I had my own ideas. I had my own reasons. I made my own decisions.

Even though I didn't always listen I longed to please her

and wanted her to be happy. I knew she loved me and was proud of my accomplishments, but my inability to find satisfaction and stability in my personal life weighed on her. She wanted better for me. She wanted me to be happy. She wanted us to be closer.

IN THE POTTER'S HANDS

Sometimes in the battles of life, you lose a little ground. I did. From the altar at the Methodist Church to the altar at my Grandma's church I steadily grew in faith and obedience. From the altar in my Grandma's church to the altar where I made my marriage vows I put my faith to work and shared my faith with everyone I could.

My husband sang in a gospel group that traveled to churches and schools across the United States and Canada. I went with them and as people knelt at the altars, I shared scriptures and hope and prayed with them. Many gave their lives to the Lord and many burdens were lifted. The Lord was answering my prayers. He was using me. He was using us.

After a few years, most of the members of the group had married and were finding other areas of ministry. My husband led worship at our church. It was the perfect time to start the family I wanted so badly. That was when things started falling apart.

Before I married, I always said I would only marry once. There would be no divorce for me. But sometimes life catches you by surprise. I had high expectations for myself and life, but I didn't know how to handle disappointments.

38

You might call it pride. We had busy lives like everyone else. But when I felt neglected in my marriage I didn't ask for help. I should have prayed and stayed. But I didn't. I feared my marriage was failing and began to doubt if I would ever have a family. I made selfish choices, huge errors in judgment and fell flat on my face.

As time passed, I found myself struggling to get back to what was I knew was right. Without my Christian friends, I was weak. I compromised my standards, and for many years, did not represent my faith well. It seemed no matter how hard I tried, I could not find satisfaction in life. Eventually, I began to question what was true.

But God never lets go. Like a father longing to mend a relationship with his child, He waits.

Thankfully, I have come full circle. I know what is true and have the proof. It is the peace in my heart!

> *Then I went down to the potter's house, and there he was, making something at the wheel. And the vessel that he made of clay was marred in the hand of the potter; so he made it again into another vessel, as it seemed good to the potter to make.*

> *Jeremiah 18:3-4*

The truth is none of us are perfect. We are in the Potter's hands. He desires to make us into something He can use.

The Beginning
of the End

✠

Four Years or So

MOTHER'S DAY POEM 2003

BEAUTIFUL MOTHER

One that has been with me the longest
Caring, nurturing, protecting from the start.
It is when I hear the music in your voice
That I feel a joy within my heart.

And you may not know how much
I want you to be happy,
For many times I caused you pain
While following my passions.

Somehow it seems we've found a time
When more often that I call
Your tone has that melodic ring
That warms my heart the most of all.

Looking back, I wonder if the improvement in our
relationship was partly due to the beginning of changes in
her personality. She didn't seem as critical, just happy.

MARTY'S FIRST CHILD

By 2004, my sister, Marty, was the only one of us who
didn't have children and it was time. She seemed to have
more than enough of everything else. Our little sister has
always been kind and understanding, never mean to
anyone. She is slim and smiling, always wearing the latest

43

styles. Marty has oodles of friends, and at that time, was living in a million dollar home on a golf course they owned with her husband's family.

I often wondered how a girl who thought cornflakes grew on trees could achieve such a level of prosperity while the rest of us lived our humble lives. She also believed bunnies laid eggs. This was a direct influence of the Cadbury commercials that ran on TV around Easter. I've accused her of being silly to make us laugh, but she insists, "No, I really thought bunnies laid eggs."

We all wanted so much for her to complete her dream. She was finally, pregnant.

Braxton was born in February of 2005, but something was wrong. The nurse brought him to the window for us to see. They had him wrapped up tight in a blanket and we were so happy to see him and couldn't wait for our turn to hold him, but something didn't feel right. The words weren't flowing right. Then they told us there were problems. His little arm wasn't formed properly. "Well, we can do a lot with one arm! That won't be a problem," we all agreed. "We've waited for this little guy! We love him! It'll be okay."

But then they told us he's not taking fluids like he should. We weren't prepared for this. If he can't eat, what can they do? Surely this is just a temporary condition. They decided to take him to the children's hospital for testing, so we called for prayer requests and migrated to Little Rock. We all hurt for Marty and David. We were all devastated. But we weren't quitters. We would get through this.

Braxton was diagnosed with CdLS (Cornelia de Lange Syndrome), and we were stunned to learn this could mean a shortened life expectancy, feeding tubes, possible deafness, heart problems, and even reduced mental functioning. It was heartbreaking. We so wanted Marty to enjoy being a mother, and this was going to be a challenge. But love would get us through.

It was only a few days until we found out that Braxton also had a serious heart defect. Because of the CdLS, he would not qualify for surgery. We all took our turns holding and loving and rocking and talking to this sweet little one, knowing our time with him would be short. And so they took him home and a few days later, while cradled in his daddy's arms, Jesus took Braxton home. He had lived only thirteen days. We all loved him so much.

So we worried about Marty. I tried to pray, but words became wails. It is impossible to understand why something like this happens.

We just have to trust, I reminded myself.

> *Trust in the Lord with all your heart, and lean not on your own understanding; in all your ways acknowledge Him, and He shall direct your paths.*
>
> *Proverbs 3:5-6*

A ROUGH YEAR

Recently, I asked my sister, Jack, when she first noticed something was wrong with Mama. She recalled conversations with Mama at the hospital in Little Rock during the time Braxton was there. They were making arrangements for rides back and forth to the hospital and Mama was confused about whose car they were taking and who was driving. It just didn't make sense to her. Jack recalls going back to the car with her husband Rick and telling him, "Something's not right."

I asked Jackie when he first noticed problems starting. He talked about his brother, Tommy who died in 2005. Jackie's brothers and sisters were gathering at Tommy's to be with him in his last hours. It was the end of a battle with lung cancer. Mama had driven the car over and Jackie had gotten out, but she was having trouble getting it parked. He had to park it for her.

Susan recalled Thanksgiving that year. Mama disappeared to the back bedroom and came back with a grin and a small plastic reindeer. She wound it up and it began to poop tiny brown jelly beans on the table. She thought it was funny. We were a little surprised at the time. This was not normal for our proper mother. Looking back, Susan's husband Bill says, "I knew your mom was losing it when she thought that deer pooping jelly beans was funny."

One day, Mama called home from the grocery store to tell Jackie she had lost her purse with her wallet and her keys in it. She needed a ride home. He called Steve to go get her, but by the time he got there, she had already gone. A store employee had recovered the purse. It was found in the fruit and vegetable isle. She sat it down while she was shopping and forgot about it. When she got home, she gave Jackie the keys. That was the last time she drove.

For both Mama and Jackie, 2005 was emotionally hard. It took a toll on them and early in December, in the middle of the night, I got a call from Mama. She said, "I called an ambulance for Jackie. I think he's having a stroke. They're taking him to the hospital. Can you go and meet him there?"

"Yes, but are you riding with him?" I asked as I grabbed for clothes in the dark.

"Steve is on his way over. I'll wait for him and he can take me," she said.

Somehow, I beat the ambulance to the hospital and took care of what paperwork I could. When they brought him in, Jackie's blood pressure was very low and he was unresponsive. He was so pale. The doctor was there soon after he arrived and was able to treat him in time to keep the damage to a minimum. Thank God!

Within a couple of days, he was much improved. Still, his left side was weak and he had to concentrate on his swallowing. He stayed in the hospital for a few days and then was moved to rehab where he stayed for a couple of weeks.

During that time, Marty spent a lot of time with her dad. She was his second set of ears making sure we understood everything and were getting him the things he needed. But he was missing Mama. She wasn't involved like she should have been. Susan brought her to visit, but she wasn't on top of things like she should have been. It was obvious,

47

now, to him that Mama had changed. At home in the usual routine, these subtle changes were not so evident.

We were happy that Jackie was able to come home in time for Christmas. In the weeks after the holidays, Marty drove him to physical therapy appointments and gave him the encouragement he needed. He continued to improve and today, the only reminder of the stroke is a bit of weakness in his grip and a little numbness in his left hand. He has had an amazing recovery from the stroke. We are so thankful.

MAKING SENSE OF IT ALL

My sister, Susan, was on the trail for a diagnosis long before I began to hear the alarm. She called me. "What's wrong?" I asked.

"She's tired and forgetful, and doesn't want to do anything anymore. I've been coming over and paying the bills for her."

"I knew you were helping, but I thought you were just trying to help her straighten out a few things," I needed clarification.

"When I started, that's what I did, but now I take care of it all," Susan explained. "She has trouble balancing the checkbook and she doesn't want to go shopping anymore. I've been ordering things from the catalog for her."

"Can she still write a check?"

"Yes. What do you think we should do? She's tried taking ginkgo, ginger, and fish oil. But we can't tell if any of it is helping."

"Okay. Let me think about this. She's only 62. This shouldn't be happening," I sighed.

So the next time I visited, I made a point to take Mama shopping. We went to the chicken outlet to pick up frozen chicken strips. I was concerned at how long it took for her to write out a check. She slowly formed each letter as if she were copying her own signature from memory. Then on the way to the car, she took way too long to get down the curb. The word surefooted came to mind. And she was not.

Susan thought it could be hormones. I agreed. Mama's doctor had taken her off hormone replacement therapy (HRT) when a new study was released saying it could be bad for your heart. We wondered if that could have caused her hormones to get out of whack. So Susan took her to a local pharmacy that tested for hormone imbalance. They gave her progesterone cream to rub on her tummy. After a few months of this, we couldn't see any difference.

 Next I scheduled her for an ultrasound of the carotid arteries through Lifeline screening. There was a screening taking place about an hour away, in Oklahoma. So we planned to have lunch while we were out and enjoyed the drive. They checked for aneurisms and blockage in her arteries. In a few weeks we got the report. No problems there.

So we switched from her general practitioner to a geriatric

physician thinking someone who specialized in treating the elderly would be more likely to help us find some answers. We asked if she could be having mini-strokes or if she could have had a stroke. The doctor agreed that it could have been a stroke, but explained that you can't always tell for sure. When we asked Mama if she remembered having a stroke or feeling bad like she couldn't move, she nodded and said, "Before Thanksgiving, before Jackie had his stroke."

Jackie remembered, "There was a day she couldn't even hold her head up."

The doctor advised us that further testing for a stroke would most likely be inconclusive, and prescribed something to help prevent a stroke in the future. We chose to wait. No more testing for now.

Then one day Mama complained of chest pain, so we went to the ER. They didn't find anything wrong with her heart, but while we were there we told them about the problems we were having and about the possible stroke. They did a CT scan of her brain, but said it showed no sign of a stroke. While they were doing the CT, I peeked into the control room and saw the pictures of my mother's brain on the screen. Normally, that's just not something you would ever expect to see and I wasn't sure how I would feel about it. But what I saw was the most healthy, pink, curvy, plump picture of a brain I had ever seen. I remember thinking, "Even my Mama's brain is beautiful. Surely there isn't anything wrong with it."

WITHDRAWING

She began to withdraw socially in 2006. At first I didn't see it. I was busy with work and life and although I talked to her on the phone, I didn't see her that often. When we spent time together, we usually had an agenda, the greenhouse for flowers, or shopping for a graduation gift. She may have been a little more anxious at the holiday gatherings than normal. But I get anxious when I'm having a gathering at my house too.

When her best friend and sister-in-law, Sandy, died from breast cancer in September of 2006 she didn't want to go to the visitation. She was spending all of her time in the back room, sitting in her chair, smoking, watching soaps, Dr. Phil, and HGTV. Maybe she wanted to avoid making a mistake that would offend someone, like forgetting a name, or maybe following conversations was becoming confusing, or maybe she was just depressed. She was wringing her hands for no reason. Who really wrings their hands? We tried changing her antidepressant.

I told Susan, "Where's my mother and who is this person that has taken her place? I miss her."

"I know," she commiserated. "She doesn't have much to say about anything anymore. She doesn't give advice or tell us how things ought to be."

I chuckled, "We should be glad, but I'm not. It's just not right!"

"No, I know what you mean," Susan sadly said. "It's not

the way my Mama is. I miss her too."

Sometime in 2007, Mama stopped answering the phone. When we talked, she would get confused and hand the phone to Jackie, saying, "You tell her." And so he would tell me the recent family news and I would tell him about my days and my kids and to be honest, I started to feel a little frustrated. I love Jackie, but there were things I wanted to talk to Mama about. And I wanted her to hear my stories from *me*. We had lost something. I wanted to know what was going on.

One of the last times she actually said something to me on the phone was around Thanksgiving in 2007, when my great aunt Delphia was in rehab. She was the only one of Grandma's siblings still alive. Of all Grandma's sisters, Aunt Delphia was the most outspoken. She had travelled often in her life and actually worked during WWII in a shipyard in Oregon. She was a real live Rosie the Riveter. Even as she got older, her style could be a bit racy. As a result of her edgy personality, she often offended members of her family. Even so, we loved her and visited her often. Her daughter, Darlene was a good friend to Mama. Darlene had spoken with me and told me about finding her mother at the rehab with wet hair, cold, in bed. When I told Mama about this she began to laugh and said, "They put her to bed wet?" and just laughed.

I was appalled. Mama's standards were always high. She always told us, "If you can't say something good about someone, don't say anything at all."

And she believed, as Jesus taught, that we should treat others as we would want to be treated: with patience, kindness, and love. Her reaction to Aunt Delphia's dilemma sounded far from compassionate and not like my mother at all.

Later, as I learned more about Alzheimer's, I realized the reaction was what they call, "an inappropriate response", which is common with dementia and probably why Mama was not getting out of the house much. She would never have laughed at anyone's misfortune.

Aunt Delphia died on Christmas Eve that year as her husband had years before.

After that, when I called, I would tell Jackie my news and then I would ask him to let me talk to Mama and I would tell her when I would be coming to see her and what we would do together and would remind her that I love her.

DOING LESS

As time passed, Mama's vocabulary was shrinking, but she had no trouble hearing, and even though she found it difficult to follow instructions, she seemed to comprehend what we told her. You could say she was a good listener. Her conversations consisted mostly of listening with short responses. She didn't explain or describe anything or express her feelings anymore. Her comments were one or two sentences, or less. We began telling people that Mama had had a stroke. This made it easier for people to know how to interact with her.

It was during this time that I read a copy of *Coach Broyles' Playbook for Alzheimer's Caregivers*. It is so easy to read and is without a doubt, the most helpful of all the books I read. I tried to fit Mama into the profile for Alzheimer's disease. Some of the symptoms applied, but some didn't. She knew who we were. And she could remember what happened from day to day. But she was forgetting how to do things and she was forgetting words.

By the end of 2007, Mama wasn't cooking anymore. It was beyond disinterest. She couldn't follow a recipe or keep the burners adjusted. Jackie was getting overwhelmed. He was getting tired of sandwiches and was trying to take up the slack in the cleaning department. Mama would remind him when the laundry was beginning the rinse cycle so he could put the fabric softener in and she would help fold the clothes. One day the washer overflowed on the spin cycle. She hurried to find Jackie and with a worried look said, "Puddle."

And she was folding a lot of paper towels. Jackie showed me a growing stack of neatly folded paper towels on the trunk in the back room where she watched TV. There were a few on the end table in the living room also. She would fold them and carry them to her stack in the back. (Okay. I admit it. I did read Dr. Seuss as a child.)

She would also make the beds. But that was about it. She wasn't sewing, shopping, cooking, cleaning, or reading. I asked her why she didn't read anymore and she said "Can't keep my place. Same thing over and over."

Smoking was something we all wished she wouldn't do. Jackie quit in 2005, when he had the stroke. Two years later, she was still smoking. We didn't like it, but none of us wanted to take it from her. Maybe it helped her nerves and it was one thing she seemed to enjoy. But it got to the point where she was smoking too much. At times, she would forget she had a cigarette lit and would light a second one. When Mama finally forgot how to light her own cigarettes, Jackie told her it was time to quit and he put them away in a drawer in her sewing room.

Even watching TV was becoming difficult. She was having trouble operating the remote. She would come from the back room, remote in hand, wanting Jackie to change the channel for her. She knew what needed to be done, just forgot how to do it. He knew all her favorite shows and what time they came on.

DIAGNOSIS

We tried to figure out when the symptoms first started. Mama would be 65 in January and would qualify for Medicare. We definitely needed some help.

All the time we searched for a reason for what was happening, we knew it could be Alzheimer's disease. We talked about it once in a while, but we didn't want it to be true. So we did everything we could to prove it was something else. Something that could be fixed.

I recall, one afternoon, Mama and Jackie came over to our house for dinner. I can't remember what year, but Mama was still well, or seemed so to me. It was a beautiful day. As they walked in the front door the sun streamed in and I met her with a hug and kiss. She gave me a smile and handed me a book. This was not unusual. It was a rare occasion that a visit with Mama didn't involve a gift of some sort. Something to let you know she had been thinking of you. It could be something as simple as a recipe. But giving, or sharing, is a tradition with us. Rather than throwing things away, we pass them around and find new locations, and new functions for old items. A dress she picked up at a yard sale has become my work-in-the-garden dress, and I imagine my old house dress may someday become a doll's blanket in my daughter's house that reminds her of her mother and her grandmother.

In my hand, I held the book she had given me. It was an old copy of *The 36-Hour Day*. I silently looked at her and shook my head. Then I gave her a smile back, and said, "Uh uh," and gently sat the book on top of a stack of books that occupied the shelf beside us.

I asked Jackie, "Is she giving me this book for any particular reason?" He told me she had been to see the doctor, but since the doctor wasn't in, she had talked to the nurse practitioner who said she could have Alzheimer's.

I didn't really want to face it. I wanted our world to stay the same a little while longer. Now, as I think back I realize how I dismissed the idea. I wish I had talked about it with her and asked her what was happening. I wish I had reassured her that I would do everything in my power to take care of her. Because I knew I would. But she didn't know it. Of course I told her later, but so much time passed before I said it. There must have been many times she wondered what would become of her.

Many changes came in 2008. We began to adapt. We could no longer deny we had a big problem. We needed to know what to expect so we could prepare. We were given a new copy of *The 36-Hour Day* at the doctor's office and were referred to a neurologist.

The neurologist we went to see is very well respected in our local health systems. In fact, she was the doctor that successfully treated Jackie when he had the stroke two and a half years earlier. We were confident in her ability and hopeful to finally pin down a diagnosis. Even so, the ride to her office was a little tense. Whatever it was, we would deal with it.

I had been reading about different types of dementia. I had learned there are many possible causes of dementia: stroke, vascular disorders, Parkinson's, Picks disease, heavy metal poisoning, frontotemporal dementia (FTD), and Alzheimer's, to name a few. All result in degeneration of the brain. From my limited research, it seemed that each of these diseases had a different set of symptoms at the beginning, maybe depending on which area of the brain is affected first, but they all ended about the same.

When it was our turn, the doctor took her time with us. She used flashcards to test Mama's memory and language skills. I was surprised how many items Mama could not recall the name for. She tested her reflexes. Her legs and feet were slow to respond. She tested her comprehension and ability to follow instructions.

"Put your finger to your nose," the doctor instructed. "Okay, now take your finger off your nose and touch my finger." The doctor was holding her finger up in front of Mama. Mama took her finger off her nose and stopped mid-air in front of her face. *Did she understand?*

"Let's try it again," the doctor took Mama's finger, and placed it on Mama's nose again and then moved it slowly over to touch the finger she was still holding up.

"Now, you do it. Touch my finger with yours." It was her turn. Mama gave the same response as before. Her finger stopped mid-air. *How could this be?* I guess she just forgot where she was going with it. The same way we sometimes forget why we came into a room.

The level of decline, the realization of how much we had lost already was glaringly apparent. The doctor told us Mama was suffering from semantic dementia and that it was progressing rapidly. She described it as similar to Alzheimer's, but that the front portion of the brain is more severely affected and that her language and decision making abilities would continue to decline. She summed it up, "She will eventually forget how to do everything and will require 24/7 care."

The neurologist had been very respectful of Mama during her examination. And she was very kind to us as she explained, "There is nothing you could have done to prevent this from happening and there is nothing you can do to stop it."

The doctor left us to gather her notes and we began to absorb what we had just seen and heard. We reassured Mama that we would help her and take good care of her. But she was handling this better than Jackie and me. She seemed satisfied that, finally, we knew what she couldn't tell us.

The doctor prescribed Aricept and explained that it might

slow down the progression of the disease and bring back a slight level of functionality. She promised us a month's worth of Aricept to get us started. Then she released us to the waiting room to pick up the samples. It was so crowded in there it was standing room only. While we waited, it hit me how much our lives had changed. It didn't matter that we had been chasing a diagnosis for three years. It still hit me like a ton of bricks. Tears began to stream down my face. I couldn't stop it. I was overwhelmed. The dam broke and my emotions rolled free.

I whispered to Jackie, "I'll be right back," and I headed for the door and the cover of my Jeep where I could cry. I felt terrible leaving them in the waiting room by themselves, but could hold it no longer. For some reason, on this occasion, reality refused to be pushed aside. I had to face what I couldn't bear to think about, that my beautiful, loving mother was ruined and dying. But, I was determined to go through it with her no matter how painful.

There was also a realization that I would be sacrificing time with my husband and my children, to care for my mother. Later, my husband, Glenn said, "It wasn't a sacrifice. It was an act of love."

Even though it seems selfish to think of what we must give up, we all have our plans and dreams and when tragedy happens, we have to decide to let some things go. I'm thankful my husband gave me support for what I wanted to do.

PICKING UP WHERE SHE LEFT OFF

I was spending more and more time at Mama and Jackie's and getting more involved in their life. The more time I spent there, the more I saw what needed to be done. There comes a time when you realize that she isn't going to be cleaning or cooking anymore and you can't ignore it any longer. I wanted to help with the cooking and asked Jackie if I could fix something different for them to eat. At first he said no, they were doing okay, but I could tell by the look in Mama's eyes, she was ready for some home cooked meals.

So I got more specific, "How about some meatloaf or a pot of beans with ham, and cornbread?"

I could tell he was considering it. "Well, Mama would probably like some meatloaf with peas and mashed potatoes."

So I would cook for them once in a while. I made the meals Mama made for us when I was still at home, I made tortilla surprise, and hamburger and macaroni and cheese casserole, and with a little help from one of Mama's cookbooks I even managed chicken and dumplings.

As I cooked, I began to clean out the cabinets. There were outdated sauces, and a box of macaroni and cheese with weevils. I had no idea. They had been making do for a long time. I was a little surprised, because I remember Jackie helping with dinners when I lived at home and wondered why he hadn't been cooking more. Things had come to a standstill. Finally, we talked about it.

He was discouraged and sad that it had come to this. He was reluctant to take on the responsibility of the meals, first, because he was sad that he needed to, because Mama couldn't do it anymore. And second, because he had a lot to learn. They had often cooked together, but he rarely had the run of the kitchen.

Susan and I began to encourage him to try different things. We explained how important it was for them to eat more vegetables, to eat healthy. We told him he could call us if he needed instructions and showed him how easy it was to make cornbread and pancakes from a mix. Soon he was cooking again. He made roast with potatoes and carrots on Sunday, and fried pork chops and baked country style ribs with barbeque sauce.

One day he came home from the store with a package of salad greens saying, "Mama used to love salad."

He is such a trooper.

TYING UP LOOSE ENDS

Susan has been a stay at home Nana for years. She and Bill have six granddaughters and one grandson. She takes care of her grandchildren while their mommies and daddies are at work. It seems that about the time one gets old enough for school another one or two come along. So her weeks are busy, but she has been going over to Mama and Jackie's on Sundays to pay the bills since 2005. She was very aware of the changes in Mama's abilities. She was ready to get some things taken care of.

We talked about living wills, funeral arrangements, and if we needed power of attorney. But we kept putting it all off. We didn't want Mama to have to face it. We knew her wishes from conversations in recent years, but it was not put down on paper. Finally, we decided to get all those things done. We had put them off longer than we should have. It was time to deal with them so we wouldn't have to think about it again.

We all agreed that Susan should be on the checking account. That was easy enough.

Then Susan, Jackie, Mama, and I gathered at the kitchen table and helped Mama sign a Living Will. We explained to her, "This means we won't keep you alive with a feeding tube or life support. When it's your time to go, it's your time."

She nodded.

We agreed I would be the Healthcare Proxy, which would let me make decisions about her care if something were to happen to Jackie. Then we helped her sign it. She really couldn't sign her name at that time. So we wrote her signature down for her, so she could look at it and copy. When I had to hold her hand and help her, I think we all realized we had waited longer that we should have. It was never notarized. And, thankfully, we never needed power of attorney. It was just a formality for us. A point in time where we faced what was ahead and agreed on a plan. It was a promise.

A little later, we made an appointment with a representative from the funeral home and took care of the arrangements. Susan and Jackie told me they had discussed, with Mama, a few years ago, what her wishes for final arrangements were. Mama was at the table with us through all the discussions and arrangements. I was surprised to hear she wanted to be cremated and didn't want an open casket at the visitation or the funeral. I worried that some of the grandchildren might want to see her one last time. But I think she knew what this disease would do and worried that she wouldn't look like herself. What she didn't know was how much her family would love her and care for her to the very end.

DECISIONS ABOUT MEDICATIONS

At the time of diagnosis, Mama was taking an antidepressant, a water pill, a blood pressure pill, a heart regulator, something for cholesterol, a baby aspirin, and ibuprofen. She was taking 800mg of ibuprofen three times a day for arthritis in her knees and back. I was alarmed at the dosage, knowing she had been taking it at this rate for several years and I encouraged her to take it only if she needed it. But she wanted it all the time. I had heard of studies that showed regular use of ibuprofen could reduce chances of getting Alzheimer's, but obviously it wasn't working for her. At this point, I was more concerned about liver damage, or bleeding in the digestive tract. Evidently, Mama had a stomach made of iron. Eventually, we would try backing off on the ibuprofen. But when we did, she started having some pain in her knees. It was helping with inflammation in her joints. So we let her keep taking it.

To be honest, I was still looking for something that could be causing the dementia. So I examined anything that could cause a side effect or symptom. Anything used in excess or any deficiency.

Susan had been bringing fish oil for Mama to take for a while. We agreed she should continue to take the fish oil, to help keep cholesterol levels good and for the brain.

And we added the Aricept. When you start taking Aricept, you increase the dosage gradually each week and watch for side effects. We made it through the first thirty days of samples with no problems. So we filled the prescription. A week later, Mama started crying. She was experiencing a tremor in her left arm. It would get rigid and shake uncontrollably and she would cry. Bless her heart. It was more than she could handle. We just cried with her. I remember my daughter, Aja, sitting by Nanny's chair, holding her hand while she cried. Aja is one of the strongest women I know and rarely cries, but her eyes overflowed that day. I'm sure Aja had never seen Nanny cry before. It was heartbreaking.

As the days passed, the tremors became worse. They were occurring every few hours and would last twenty or thirty minutes. We asked her if it hurt, but she couldn't tell us. We called the doctor's office. They told us what to do to help her relax. We tried movement, but it didn't seem to help. She tried to hold her arm still with her other hand, but the tremors persisted. So we stopped taking the Aricept. The day after she stopped taking it, there were only three short occurrences of the tremors and the second day after we stopped, only one. Then the tremors went away. It had been a week since they started.

But something else was happening. I suppose once Mama got started crying, she couldn't stop. I don't know if the tremors had scared her, or if something else was happening in her mind. Maybe the Aricept changed something in her mind, maybe not. But she was upset. As far as we could tell, she wasn't having hallucinations, but she was very anxious. Maybe she realized the pills weren't going to help as she had hoped. She began to let it all out.

We called the doctor and were given a prescription for Abilify. Abilify is an antipsychotic medication that comes with a warning of possible sudden death for patients with dementia. We decided not to fill it. It might have helped, but after our experience with Aricept, we weren't ready to start anything new yet. It didn't help that she couldn't tell us what was going on. We decided to give her some time. We recognized things would change as the disease progressed and hoped this stage would pass quickly.

Soon, my visits to Mama and Jackie's house would start with updates on what had happened since I was there last. I would sit on the couch with Mama while Jackie recounted her episodes. I remember him painfully describing Mama sitting in the middle of her bed, crying out as loud as she could. It was as if she were calling on God with all her heart. I'm sure she was.

IN BETWEEN THE TEARS

The weather was warm now, so Mama and Jackie came to visit me at work. The view of the Ozark Mountains was beautiful from the Christian ministry where I worked. We walked from the office down past the house to take in the scenery from the gazebo. On the way back I asked Mama if she wanted to walk over to see the retreat center. She was walking slowly. I asked if the exercise might help loosen things up.

She shook her head.

"Is it too far to walk?"

She shook her head.

"Is it your knees or your hips?" I asked. Jackie said her arthritis had been bothering her and it made it painful to walk. I told her I was so sorry she had to go through this.

"I guess it's just my lot," she said, without a hint of anger.

I remember Mother's Day 2008. Mama and Jackie came to my house for dinner. Susan and Bill were there and my kids. It was a perfect day except for a moment of panic when I realized she was changing. Her expressions were different. She had just started the Aricept. Maybe it was the medicine. I grabbed the camera and took Mama by the arm. I was anxious to capture what was left of her. I didn't really think it was the medicine. The disease was starting to take a toll on her body.

I wondered how bad it was - what she was really capable of. I wondered if she would enjoy doing something if I helped her. She loved sewing, so I looked for something familiar. In her sewing room was a small chest of drawers full of colorful spools of thread, ric rac, patches, ribbon, crochet needles, knitting needles, pin cushions, eyes for dolls, and a machine for putting studs on purses and t-shirts. The old bookshelf was full of neatly folded fabric. On the top were boxes of patterns and a row of craft books. My eyes wandered back to the chest. She had three antique Mason jars full of buttons just waiting for a purpose. I threaded an oversized needle with some colorful embroidery thread thinking to put her to work stringing buttons. First we sorted them. She liked looking at the buttons and picked them up and moved them around. Then we tried stringing them. I helped her get started, but I don't think she knew what to do. She seemed bored.

As I put away the buttons, I admired the double wedding ring quilt Mama and Grandma had made together years ago. It hung on a wooden quilt rack Jack's husband, Ricky had built. The quilt covered a big part of the wall in front of her sewing area where she could enjoy it while she stitched.

I remembered the wonderful rugs she used to crochet out of strips of material torn from old sheets or curtains. I always wanted to learn. There was plenty of material. So I decided to make a rug. I began to cut the strips. She watched me for a while and then reached for the fabric. I handed it to her and she folded it and gave it back to me. Of course! With the fabric folded in half I would have half the cutting to do. It was always a happy moment when we could see her mind at work. I read her rug making book and was reminded how to make a slit in the end of each strip and string them together. So I did the cutting and strung them together and she rolled the long strips up into a ball. Then I had to remember how to crochet. She showed me how when I was a girl, but that was a long, long time ago. I looked at the rug book again. Trying to decipher the instructions was not as easy as watching someone do it. So I put it in her hands and she slowly crocheted a row. I tried it, with some success, but I didn't know how to make the curve. So I handed it back to her. She showed me how to make two stitches in one loop so the rug wouldn't buckle as it grew. So the center of the rug had Nanny's stitches in it. Our material was solid pink and taupe, and some calico with pink flowers. When it was finished, we decided it would belong to the next baby girl born in our family.

I got her to help me with small tasks in the kitchen, like peeling carrots. It was good to have her in the kitchen. When we were doing dishes she was the rinser. She was very slow, but the warm water felt good to her. And she felt useful. She often walked away from a task in the middle of it, but that was okay. Papa would tease her about getting fired for walking off the job and she would smile. We warned her to stay away from the stove, just to be on the safe side.

A WEDDING

In September, my daughter, Aja, got married. It was a beautiful day. We had planned and worked all summer. It was a sunny, country wedding on the lawn behind the old house Mike's great-grandpa had built. Pictures of Mike and Aja as children and as a couple hung on the clothesline. Mason jars of wildflowers, basil, and white roses topped the tables. Kids blew bubbles and danced to the live Celtic band as friends and family gathered. And Aja was beautiful, radiant strolling across the green lawn, blue, blue sky behind her.

Mama was there, happy. She gazed proudly as Aja, made her promises. Of course, we had missed her during the planning of the wedding. She would have loved making the alterations on Aja's wedding dress. And she would have been a great help with the decorations and the food. I was just thankful that she could be there for this special day to watch Marty's triplets dance with Jack and Ricky's granddaughters. (Yes, Marty has a trio of boys now.)

Mike and Aja's sweet little dog Buddy was assigned the honor of ring bearer. Aja made a special collar for him just to hold the rings. During the ceremony, when it was time for him to bring the rings, Mike whistled for him and, happy to be in the middle of things, Buddy ran right up to them. Perfect! He was so cute. After the rings were delivered, ooos and aaws turned to laughter when Buddy refused to leave center stage. He decided the place for him was right there with his Mama and Daddy and with a big grin on his doggie face, he proudly made himself comfortable on the train of Aja's beautiful dress. We called him, but he wouldn't budge. Aja's cousin, Jonathan, attempted to physically remove him, but he put up a protest and looked so sad that everyone agreed, "Let him stay!" So be it.

At the end of September, Glenn's daughter, Heather, brought our grandson, Connor, for a visit. He was nine months old at the time. It was so good to see them. It was nice to hold him and to laugh together and watch him eat corn-on-the-cob for the first time. It was nice to be at the other end of the life cycle for a couple of weeks. I wished they didn't live so far away.

Christmas 2008 I was taking pictures again. Mama was laughing at everything I said. Laughter is good, but finally, Jackie gently told her, "Mama, you don't have to laugh at everything."

THE NURSING HOME OPTION

She was forgetting things. She asked us, "What is happening to me?"

Jackie would say, "Mama, the doctor told us you have Alzheimer's." And sometimes he would say "Old Timer's" as the old timers call it around here.

One day she said she wanted to go to the nursing home. We knew she didn't want to be a burden, but we wanted to care for her at home. We knew that if the tables were turned and one of us was sick that she would do the same for us.

We realized that nursing homes or long-term care facilities serve a purpose. And the environment they create is much more comfortable than in years past. We talked about it often. If something were to happen to Jackie or me, we would most likely have to put Mama in a nursing home. We weighed our options. And we always kept that one open. But we knew that even though nursing homes have improved through the years and even though there are good people there trying to do their best to give quality care, we knew they could not provide the level of attention we were able to give Mama at home.

My mother was facing a time when she would have no control over her life or her body. She would be totally dependent on others to make decisions for her. She would be as vulnerable as a child. We start our lives as infants, incapable of caring for ourselves. And we are loved and nurtured by our families as we grow out of our limitations. Unfortunately, many of us will *end* our lives with limitations and once again be incapable of taking care of ourselves. If we are lucky, our families will again provide the safe and loving environment we need. I could not desert her now. She had cared for me all my life and now it was my turn to care for her. I prayed that God would make a way for me to be there for her. I needed financial help. I needed support from my family. I needed emotional and physical strength. I found strength in my relationship with Jesus.

I can do all things through Christ who strengthens me.

Philippians 4:13

It's hard to plan when you don't know what will happen next. You just have to trust. Take it one day at a time. I'm so thankful we were able to do it.

So when she said she wanted to go to the nursing home, we reassured her. Jackie told her, "Papa wouldn't have anything to do and Pam would have another job she probably wouldn't even like. And she'd rather be taking care of you." I nodded in agreement with a smile.

71

Later, I was helping her in the bathroom and she said, "I don't think you can do it."

THE START OF A ROUTINE

It was getting more difficult for Jackie to get things done. I needed to spend more time at their house. I knew that as time went on they would need more help. I was working for a Christian ministry that sends groups on short-term missions. I loved it. It was more than a job. It was an opportunity to serve. But as I prayed about what I should do I understood that helping Mama and Jackie was an opportunity to serve as well. I am so grateful that they understood and allowed me to gradually increase the time I could spend caring for my mother.

I started taking off work on Wednesday mornings. It was the morning they decided they would need me least. Instead of going to work, I would go to Mama and Jackie's house and help her get ready for her day. It would give Jackie a chance to get out of the house for awhile. He would go to the store, the pharmacy, or out for a walk if it was nice. By this time we were aware that it wasn't a good idea to leave her alone in the house. She really didn't bother anything she shouldn't, but we worried she would go outside and get lost.

I started helping her dress on the days that I was there. Jackie had been adjusting the water for her shower. He told me, "She can take a shower by herself, but you'll need to get the water started." So I helped her pick out something to wear and got the water going. I tried to give her as much privacy as possible and gave her the opportunity to do things for herself as long as she could.

I soon discovered she liked to change clothes. She would change two or three times a day. Like an adolescent. And she forgot there was a place for dressing. When she got too warm, she would start to come out of her sleeves. It didn't matter where we were. Papa would tell her to go in the bedroom to change. We tried to limit dressing to the bedroom and the bathroom.

She couldn't tell us if she needed to go to the bathroom. At times it would catch us (and I think her) by surprise. Jackie and Mama had been going to Marty's house on most Saturday mornings since the triplets were born; however, lately not so often. The boys were nearly three years old now. One day at Marty's, Mama was looking anxiously around the kitchen, so Marty asked her if she needed to go to the bathroom, thinking to point her in the right direction. Mama didn't answer; she just started to pull down her pants. They hurried her to the bathroom, but after that, Jackie was reluctant to take her out by himself, not knowing what was going to happen next.

It was around this time that Jackie started referring to himself as Papa in relation to Mama, like he did with the grandkids. It was his way of adapting to the new role of caregiver and it seemed appropriate to us. Things would never be the same. He had to let go of the past and accept things as they were. She no longer did the things a wife does. She was just "Papa's little girl."

She was having trouble picking out what clothes to wear. I tried to make it easier for her by laying out two outfits and letting her pick. She was having a little trouble lining up her buttons and sometimes she would try to put her shoe on the wrong foot. She liked to change shoes and did it often. They didn't always match. As long as it wasn't hurting anything, we let her do her thing. At least she was *doing* something. So what if she wanted to brush her teeth three times a day and go to the potty three times in an hour.

I started styling her hair with the blow dryer and round brush. She wasn't doing anything with her hair at all. I realized how much Jackie had been helping her with grooming. It was a little awkward at first, but I got better at it. Sometimes when I was finished with her hair, she would stand in front of the mirror and look it over and then tuck her hair behind her right ear.

Soon I started taking two days off each week to help, then three. We had a pretty good routine. Mama and Jackie were usually eating breakfast when I arrived. After breakfast, I helped Mama with her shower, helped her get dressed, and fixed her hair. Then we made the beds and if Jackie hadn't done them yet, we did the dishes. After that we would plan lunch or find something to clean or straighten. One day, I was in the living room brushing the dust off the back of the couch when she came up beside me and put her hand on the couch and said, "Who'd have thought."

I said, "What, that I'd be cleaning in *your* house or that you would ever let it get this bad?" And I had a realization. *My once confident, capable mother still knows so much.*

If it was nice in the afternoon, we sat on the front porch in the wicker rocking chairs. One such day, as we sipped our water, she said, "A little lighter."

I pondered a few moments, "Yes, I had a little lighter at one time and I left it here, but I took that home a long time ago."

She said it again, "A little lighter," and this time she looked right at my pudgy waistline.

"Oh! I see! You think I should be a little lighter!" I paused. "Yes, mother. I promise, I will work on it just for you."

Mama liked to have a snack around ten o'clock in the morning and she would have another snack around two o'clock in the afternoon. It seemed she lived to eat. I was bad about working in the kitchen with only the light from the windows. She would say, "Why don't you… turn on the light." And I would be so happy she said something I would thank her profusely and tell her how much it helped to have the light on. One day she said, "Why don't you… cook something simple."

I couldn't believe my ears. *Cook something simple!* It was good to hear her come up with a new sentence. She would go days without saying anything but "Yeah" and "Okay." On this occasion, I think she was hungry.

After every meal, and even the snacks, she wanted to brush her teeth. She had a partial, which she would take out and lay beside the sink. I would brush the partial while she brushed her teeth. There was something about handling someone else's teeth that gave me the heebie geebies. Don't ask me why. It was just one of those things. But it didn't take long to get over it. I noticed she wasn't being thorough when brushing her teeth, so I offered to help once in a while. I watched her put in her partial. *What will we do when she forgets how to put that in?*

I decided to learn how while she could still help.

HER VOICE

As the weather got nicer, I decided to paint the utility room. They bought the paint, I supplied the labor. Mama helped us pick a rosy mauve. Pink. First I caulked; then I primed. It made Mama a little nervous to have things out of place. I worried about her tripping on something. At that time she was still spending quite a bit of time in the back room watching TV, but that was changing.

I looked through their cassette tapes for something to listen to and found Olivia Newton John's, *Have You Never Been Mellow*. When I was a teenager at home, I had a few of her records. I wanted something to sing along with while I worked. So I put it on and got back to work. I had the washer and dryer pulled out and was on my knees behind them painting the baseboards. As I painted, the songs took me back to a time when our lives were ahead of us and we were closer. And Mama was whole. I tried not to let Mama know, but I left a lot of tears back there behind the washer and dryer.

We listened to a little of everything while I painted. We played some Southern gospel music by the Hinsons, and the Happy Goodmans, and Alan Jackson's *Precious Memories* album, and Nat King Cole, and Elvis. While I was going through the tape collection, I came across a case that had the word "Me" written on it in Mama's handwriting. I had no idea what was on it, so I showed it to her and told her I was going to take it home and listen to it. I didn't want to cry in front of her and I had cried enough for one day. She didn't seem to mind, so I took it home. It was a recording of Mama playing the piano and singing "The Star Spangled Banner" and "When Johnnie Comes Marching Home". Later we found a newspaper clipping of a Veteran's Day event where Mama and a friend from church sang those songs. I was so thrilled to have her voice. Her sweet soprano. I told her she did a wonderful thing.

Living with Dementia

About Two Years

OUR WITS END

The tremors eventually came back. They weren't as strong as the ones she had the year before when she was taking Aricept, but they were upsetting her. In fact, they were so subtle that at first we didn't know what was upsetting her. She became very anxious, pacing, and crying, and screaming. But she had no tears.

At first she would only do this when she was alone with Jackie. He said she would get upset and scream until she wore herself out. It usually happened in the evening, but not every day. Sometimes a week would pass quietly. He began to let the neighbors know what was going on in case they heard her. We kept the windows closed. It was hard to take. It's unnerving to hear someone you love in such agony.

We tried to figure out what was causing her to scream, we questioned her, but she couldn't give an answer. She wouldn't nod or agree or speak. So I decided to reassure her about everything. If it was how we were treating her, we would try to do better. I knew we were treating her well, but was afraid in her mind she might think otherwise. She was funny about some things - like her water. She carried a blue plastic cup that held 20 ounces of water and would drink it until it was gone and then at the bottom, she would slurp the last of it with the straw. That was our cue to refill the cup. But she had no idea how much she was drinking, so we had to limit the refills to six or so a day. Once, she said, "Pay attention to me." If she had been in her right mind, she would have known Papa and me were giving it all we had.

We wondered if she was hallucinating. *What if she is afraid of what will happen to her?* I would tell her, "Whatever you are thinking or seeing it's not true, everything is fine, we're all safe, and we love you and we will take good care of you."

Poor Jackie. He tried holding her. He tried to comfort her. Finally, since nothing else seemed to help, he tried to ignore her. His brother Charlie told him, "I'd scream too, if this were happening to me. Just let her scream." So we did. Jackie would turn his hearing aid down and let her go on with her pacing and screaming. One day I came in at the end of one of these times. It was so awful to see her like that. I dropped my things and just held her in the middle of the living room while she screamed. To me it sounded like, "I just can't take it any more." A couple of times she pinched Jackie on the side while he held her. We told her gently not to hurt Papa. She tried so hard to be good.

I determined to spend more time with them. Jackie needed help. It was time. Otherwise, I was afraid we would have to put Mama in a nursing home. I didn't know how much of this he could take. But he was tougher than I thought.

We talked to the doctor about different kinds of medicine, but were afraid to try anything. How would we know how it made her feel? She couldn't tell us anything.

How could this be happening? It hurt so much to watch her go through this. I could tell when I arrived the next

82

day if she had cried the night before. She would be tired. And it seemed she was sleeping less. For a few days she would have endless nervous energy, no need for sleep, continually pacing the floors and wanting food to fuel the activity, then she would crash and sleep during the day and we hesitated to wake her even for meals. We would just let her rest. At least she was peaceful while she was sleeping.

Generally, we agreed that she knew what was happening and was frustrated because she was unable to do anything about it. I would have screamed too. We all prayed. We knew it would take a miracle, and were looking for one.

I kept thinking, *tomorrow, I'll go back and she will be different.*

 And some days she would be better. I prayed for God to show me what to do to make her better. For the doctors to realize they missed something. Something that could be fixed. I prayed for a miracle.

I knew in my heart that the Creator of the universe could heal my mother in an instant. But that didn't happen. The Bible tells us there is a time to live, and a time to die. And this was her time. Even so, we didn't understand why it had to be like this. Why was she suffering? We realized we may not know the answer until we get to heaven, but what we did know is that in the grand scheme of things, the sufferings of this life are small compared to the joy we will know in heaven. As I looked through her Bible one day I found one slip of paper with a scripture reference on it. I looked it up and realized she understood this too.

For our light affliction, which is but for a moment, is

working for us a far more exceeding and eternal weight of glory, while we do not look at the things which are seen, but at the things which are not seen. For the things which are seen are temporary, but the things which are not seen are eternal.

II Corinthians 4:17, 18

I reassured Mama. "He knows all about you. The Bible says that He knew you while you were in your mother's womb and that every hair on your head is counted. Now is not the time to lose faith. We have to trust Him. He loves us. We don't understand why we have to go through this now, but we will someday. And we can be thankful that we don't have to go through it alone. We have each other. And the Holy Spirit is with us. We have hope."

For You formed my inward parts; You covered me in my mother's womb.

Psalms 139:13

Are not two sparrows sold for a copper coin? And not one of them falls to the ground apart from your Father's will. But the very hairs of your head are all numbered. Do not fear therefore; you are of more value than many sparrows.

Matthew 10:29-31

ONE DAY AT A TIME

When he was having a sad day, Jackie would lay his head

down on the table holding Mama's hand and tell her, "Papa can't fix it."

It's easy to get depressed when someone you love is hurting. It's normal to be sad. You have a good reason to be sad, especially if your wife or mother is literally losing her mind one memory at a time. It helps sometimes, to have something to do. And we had plenty to do. We decided that as long as we could make her smile and keep her comfortable we could do this, one day at a time.

We found that even though we couldn't fix it, we could make the best of our situation and be thankful for each day. You have to count your blessings.

> *Be joyful always; pray continually; give thanks in all circumstances, for this is God's will for you in Christ Jesus.*
>
> *I Thessalonians 5:16-18*

We were thankful she didn't seem to be in much physical pain. And she could still walk and enjoy music and food and sunshine. I started taking her out of the house more.

GETTING OUT AND MAKING THE BEST OF THINGS

As we cleaned and cooked, she began to lose interest in her TV shows. The more we went places, the more she wanted to go. We started out making quick trips to the store if we needed something for a recipe. I put perfume and lipstick on her and dressed her up in her jewelry. I told her how beautiful she looked. And then before we went out the door, Papa would always fuss over her and tell her again how pretty she was.

One day I was looking for something different to put on her. I opened a jewelry box on the end of the dresser and it was filled with her old costume jewelry. She had sorted it into Ziploc bags with handwritten notes, "from the 50s", "I wore this with a black turtleneck", and "from the 80s." I wondered how long she had known what was happening to her.

The smaller stores were easier for us, but once we went to the mall to buy a sweater and a house dress. She still looked pretty good, and sometimes at the checkout people would speak to her directly. Sometimes she would smile, but sometimes she would look away and I would tell them, "She has Alzheimer's and can't speak." It was a little awkward at times. Most people understood, but some people just didn't know what to do. I guess they weren't sure of her capabilities.

She was forgetting how to get in the car. She was very slow. She would hesitate, and then raise the wrong foot, so I would help position her by placing her hands where they needed to be for support and then I would reach behind her left knee to remind her to lift it first. Then she would slowly get in and scoot over. Then I would fasten her belt for her. You expect to do this for a child, but when it's your mother who has been so capable all her life it's hard. And it takes patience. One day at Dollar General, I stood by in the rain while she got situated. I hoped she wouldn't see my tears mixed with the raindrops

86

on my cheeks.

The hardest part about being out in public is the people that don't want to deal with it. They ignore you and scurry off in their perfect world. I think we all do that at times. There were a couple of people that, I'm sure, thought I was crazy for bringing her out. I'm sure they thought she should have been in a nursing home. It breaks your heart, because even though she has forgotten how to do many things, she still knows what is going on.

One day we went to the grocery where Mama used to go so often. I noticed she looked especially happy as she smiled proudly at the people working in the produce department. As we passed the deli, a little lady pushing her shopping cart offered an interpretation, blurting out, "My daughter is helping me." And she just kept on rolling by. It seemed a little strange at the time. How could she have known? I do look very much like my mother.

A considerate young man at the Co-op helped us buy some seeds for the garden. He spoke to Mama and when she didn't respond as expected, I told him about the dementia. He said she reminded him of his grandmother and continued to include Mama in the conversation by making comments directed at her from time to time that didn't require a response. It really brightened our day to be treated normal. I thanked him for his help and for being so kind.

We went to the library where I checked out books on dementia and stories about sons and daughters caring for their parents. It helped to know someone else had gone through the same things we were going through. It helped to get an idea what may be coming next. How far down the road were we? I particularly enjoyed *The House on Beartown Road*, by Elizabeth Cohen. I couldn't help but laugh as I read about her life with her toddler and her elderly father. We also visited the Alzheimer's Association. They loaded us up with reading materials and invited us to support groups and meetings. I never attended the support group. I really tried to give Mama all the time I could. But I did read. I researched on the internet. I watched videos on YouTube describing Alzheimer's disease and videos of people caring for their loved ones. I encouraged Jackie to go to meetings, but he declined. He preferred to talk to his brothers and sisters, and his neighbors and friends. You have to talk to someone.

We talked to each other too. We reported to each other what we had been doing, who came to visit, what Mama had eaten, what she said, if she went to the bathroom, and why she had changed clothes. We talked about how we were feeling, if it was too much to bear, and if we were getting enough sleep. And we brainstormed about whatever the new problem was and how we could fix it. Sometimes I would go home and lie awake at night thinking about what we were going to do about something, and when I would get back to their house the next day, Jackie would have it all figured out. Sometimes we would both come to the same conclusion.

GETTING WORSE

Things evolve. Like getting up in the middle of the night. At one point, back when she would still get her own drinks, Jackie would wake up at midnight or two in the morning and Mama would be drinking coffee. The coffee pot was ready to go, all she had to do was push the button to start it. He would tell her, "Mama, it's not time to get up yet. Let's go back to bed." And she would let him lead her back to bed. We decided either she couldn't tell time any more or she didn't care what time it was, and she was going to make the most of every minute. But a few times when Jackie got up, he looked around for Forrest, their little Yorkie, and he would be outside. She had let him out, but had forgotten to let him back in. Once or twice the front door was standing open. Knowing she was opening the door, we started worrying that she might go outside and get lost. So Jackie found a deadbolt that you could lock with a key from the inside and in the evening when she started her pacing, he would tell her, "No more going outside today." And he would lock the door for the night. He put a trunk in front of the outside door in the back room. She never used that door, so we didn't worry about her going out that way. And the sliding glass door in the dining room had a stick wedged in it at night to keep it from opening and she had forgotten how to unlock it. So now, she couldn't get outside while Jackie was asleep.

The pacing and anxiety always got worse in the late afternoon. They call it sundowners. During this time she seemed more disoriented and confused and was more likely to stumble. We moved a few things that were obviously a hazard, but tried to keep things like she had them for the most part. Changes made her anxious and fretful.

Susan noticed when she came to pay the bills on Sundays,

that any deviation from their routine got Mama's attention. Susan said when she would get there, Mama knew they were going to pay the bills, and she would head for her place at the table. If Susan stayed in the living room too long or if Susan's husband, Bill, detained Jackie in the living room, Mama would go to the living room doorway and stand waiting as if to say, "Come on, we need to get this done. Susan can't stay all day!" So they would migrate to the kitchen. Then Susan would send Mama to the bedroom to get the checkbook from her purse. Susan wrote the checks, Jackie signed them, and Mama licked the envelopes. For quite a while, when they gave her the envelopes, Mama would check to see if the address was in the window and make sure the check was signed and that all was in order before she sealed it. Even though she couldn't fix it herself, she knew if something wasn't right and would hand it back so they could fix it. Then gradually, she did less and less to help. Eventually, there were days when Susan sent her for the checkbook and she came back empty-handed. But she would still lick the envelopes.

I judged the changes in her abilities by our bed making. When I first started coming over, she made the beds with me. Except for an overlooked wrinkle here and there or the bedspread hanging low up by the pillows, everything went well. I would try to be sneaky and smooth the wrinkles when she wasn't looking. One time she looked back and said, "What a mess."

Soon, I had to start reminding her what to do next, "Pull it over on your side. Okay, now throw it up over the pillows." Then a few months later, she would only stand there and watch me. So I would put the pillows in place for her, but she would still cover the pillows. It seemed unbelievable that she could lose so much.

It reminded me of the movie, *The NeverEnding Story*, where a void of darkness called The Nothing was taking over everything. It's not supposed to happen in reality. It's just a movie.

HER ADDRESS BOOK

Mama's address book leaned against the small TV in the kitchen along with the phone books. One afternoon, as I put the phone book away, I accidentally knocked the address book to the floor. At the back of the book, a paper clip held some notes. Before putting it back on the shelf, I decided to have a look. There was a page of family names. Grandma's brothers and sisters, great-grandparents, and great-great-grandparents.

There was a letter Mama had written to her brother Troy thanking him for helping with Grandma when she had to go to the nursing home. She wrote, "As Mother always said, You are True Blue. We have been through a lot together in our efforts to care for Mother. I appreciate you so much for standing with me in that difficult time." She always looked up to her oldest brother.

Now it is your turn to be cared for, Mama, I thought.

And there was a Christmas letter from a friend at Ace Hardware thanking my mother for being a friend she could talk to and depend on.

As I looked through Mama's address book I realized it would be Aunt Lil's birthday soon. Mama always called her sister who lived in California on her birthday. Aunt Lil was in her 80s by now. I wondered how she was doing and if Lil knew what had happened to Mama. So I asked Mama if she wanted me to call her. She nodded. It was good to know Aunt Lil was doing well. There were a lot of things she could no longer do. But her daughters were helping her. We visited for a few minutes and then I told her I would hold the phone for Mama, but she would have to do all the talking. I gave her a minute. While I held the phone, I watched Mama nod her head. I could see her listening, agreeing with her eyes. And a smile let me know it was time to take the phone back.

MODESTY AND HELPING WITH PERSONAL CARE

When I started spending more time with my mother the quick hugs we were accustomed to when we were all healthy and busy were not enough. I found myself sitting beside her and tucking my arm into hers, laying my head on her shoulder, and holding her hand. It was nice to be close again. When we were in the car, I would reach over and slip my hand into hers. She would hold on and sometimes rub her thumb along mine to let me know she appreciated me. Thankfully, sometimes you don't need words to communicate.

As I helped Mama with her morning routine, I became more comfortable being around her while she was undressed. She always taught us to be modest, and practiced modesty, but in this situation it was unavoidable. I knew she would need me to help more and more as time went on. One day while she was in the shower, I asked her if she was finished so I could turn off the water for her and she said, "Yeah." She said that a lot. Yeah or okay. So I turned off the water and got her towel for her. When I pulled the curtain back and covered her with her towel, I saw she still had shampoo in her hair and it was running in her eyes. After that we bought some baby shampoo. No more tears.

And I started checking on her and reminding her of what to do at each step, "Be sure to rinse your hair. Did you wash your bottom yet?"

One day after drying off, she handed me the towel. She usually hung it on the towel rack herself. I said, "Want me to hang it up?"

She said, "You tussle with it." Where did she get that word? Also, during this time frame, instead of answering no, she would say, "It's not necessary," which is saying a lot for a woman of few words. It was one of her favorite phrases.

I found myself prompting her at each task. I would get the deodorant out of the drawer and open it. She would take it and use it. Then I would set the powder in front of her and open it. And she would use it. Finally, one day as we stumbled through our routine, I said what had been on my mind for weeks, "Mama, when you can't do it anymore I will do it for you. Until then, I will remind you what to do. As your mind fails, I will take good care of your body, just like you do. As if it was mine. You teach me how. You

93

train me." I hesitated to say it, because saying it was like admitting what was coming. But I needed to tell her. I wanted her to know. Next day, she reached out of the shower with her soapy washcloth. I thought she was done with it and wanted me to rinse it for her and wring it out. But she took my hand and started washing my hand with the soapy rag. It felt nice to be cared for. I interpreted her actions to mean she would appreciate me taking care of her when the time came.

WHAT ELSE CAN GO WRONG?

We found out Mama had diabetes in September 2009. Thankfully, it wasn't too far out of control. The doctor gave her a prescription for Metformin and told us to watch her diet and get her to exercise if we could. It was the excuse I was waiting for. A reason to walk. I had been trying to get her to move, but she just wasn't interested. We adjusted her diet to include more fiber and switched to sugar free everything and I pushed a little harder for her to walk. Still she wasn't going for it. Jackie did though. Every day, weather permitting, he would get into his striped overalls, put on his hat, grab his walking cane and off he would go. He strolled through the neighborhood at a leisurely pace, taking time to visit with anyone who would talk. I told him that he needed to get his heart rate up, but he didn't care. He said "Mama used to like walking. She'd walk so fast I couldn't keep up with her, so we quit walking together." He enjoyed his strolls.

Mama, on the other hand, didn't enjoy Jackie's walks. She would pace the floors going from window to window,

94

wringing her hands, and looking. Their little Yorkie, Forrest would stand on the table by the front window until he could see Papa at the end of the driveway, then he would wag his tail and bark until he came through the door. I thought maybe Mama was worried Jackie would get hurt or wouldn't come back. I reassured her that he would be alright. That he would be back soon. Mama and Jackie had been together for 36 years and she was depending on him more and more.

Jackie's sister Susie tried to help us adjust to the sugar free diet. She told us about Braum's No Sugar Added Frozen Yogurt and when Jackie went to visit her she would send him home with delicious homemade fried raisin pies made with Splenda. We would feast on them while they were still warm and listen to Jackie tell stories about Susie's husband Bill growing tomatoes and purple hull peas in the ditch between their house and the parking lot next to them.

In the process of getting Mama set up with diabetes testing supplies and learning how to use them, we tested my husband, Glenn. His blood sugar level was sky high. He went straight to the doctor who prescribed two medications. But even with the medications and avoiding sugar and carbs like the plague, it took a week to get it down below 200. It was a good thing we found out when we did. Now we too began to adjust our lifestyle to include more regular exercise, more fiber, no sugar, and less carbs. It shook me a little, finding out Glenn had diabetes. But this was a problem we could do something about. It meant we would make the changes we needed to make anyway.

Then we got some more bad news. Dad called and told me that Sharon had collapsed. She was in the hospital and they were doing tests to find out what had caused it. I had just talked to her the week before. We were talking about what kind of vitamins they were taking and how much she loved her pets. I shook my head as I remembered Dad and his jokes. We would always go out to eat when I would visit and he would tease Sharon about her cooking. He'd say, "She thinks the smoke alarm is a timer on the stove."

It was only a few days until they found out she had lung cancer. My heart went out to them both. Dad was so lucky to have Sharon. They made it through some challenging times together. This would be the hardest.

MY HOUSE

It was around this time that I started taking Mama home with me on Friday mornings and keeping her until Saturday afternoon. It would give me a little time at home to get some things done and would give Jackie some much needed downtime. Hopefully, he would be able to get a good night's sleep. The first night Mama stayed at my house, we got all ready for bed. Teeth brushed and everything. This was a new routine for me. She was just getting into bed when she decided to say something.

 Two little tablets," she said.

I double checked her medicine. "Mama, you took all your medicine."

She was anxious and getting flustered. "Two little tablets," she said again.

So I tried another angle. "Can you tell me what the tablets are for? Show me." But she just couldn't. So I told her it would be alright we would figure it out later and tried to distract her. Next day when I took her home, I told Jackie what she had said and he didn't know what she meant. It was a mystery.

A couple of weeks later, we were getting ready to go to my house again, and Jackie told me to take the Polident and said that sometimes Mama likes to soak her teeth in it at night. He said it was expensive though so he only uses one tablet, but Mama will want to use two. Two little tablets! Now I knew what she was trying to tell me.

Packing wasn't too bad. A few outfits, her sweater, extra socks and underpants, slippers, a couple of gowns, a house dress, pads, a little bag with toothbrush, the cup for her teeth, her deodorant, and medicine. As time went on, I got her a toothbrush for my house, and deodorant, and kept a supply of pads there; even some clothes.

As I put things away in my kitchen, Mama investigated her room at my house. I had redecorated my spare room in a way that I hoped would make her feel comfortable. I put baskets on top of Grandma's old wardrobe and pulled back a new curtain with a band of feathers. In that room, we were surrounded by pictures of familiar faces, pictures of angels, and real angels. There was a table for my laptop. And my sewing machine would serve as a bedside table. "Everyone should have a sewing machine," she said when she gave it to me twenty years ago.

She wandered back into the kitchen and said, "Where's Billy?" Billy is my nephew. Susan's son. But Billy is rarely at my house. She meant to say Thomas. Our son, Thomas, was seventeen when Mama started spending Fridays and Saturdays with us. He is so easy going, respectful, and kind. I could never tell if it bothered him to share his bathroom with Nanny and he never complained about the ballgames we missed.

One day Mama and I were lying on my bed taking a rest and I was reading a book I had checked out from the library. It was a historical novel and I was telling Mama all about it. Shortly after I went back to my reading Mama made a comment about the main character that didn't make sense to me. She said, "Just wait – her baby." A week later, I finished the book and realized Mama had been telling me the ending! She had enjoyed the same book!

As we sat on the couch one Saturday morning watching a movie, I exclaimed, "That's not right!"

She turned to me matter of factly and calmly said, "It's just a movie."

I was glad Mama was spending time with me at my house. She needed a change of scenery. I thought she would enjoy being out in the country for a change. And I hoped it would satisfy her motherly concerns. I hoped she would see that I was happy. That our life is good. I believe she did see that. She looked forward to our days together at my house.

On the other hand, there were moments when it was

overwhelming. We were trying to help Mama, worrying about what Dad and Sharon were going through, and adjusting to Glenn having diabetes. It didn't help to know my paycheck was getting smaller, and that the Christmas season was approaching. We were dealing with a lot of stress.

Glenn works in retail. One Saturday morning, he was unusually quiet. I was busy with Mama and noticed he was keeping his distance, but I didn't know why. I didn't know if he was feeling bad or if he was upset about something. I tried to talk to him about it but he didn't want to talk. I didn't know if he was waiting to talk until later when Mama wouldn't be there or if he didn't want to talk to me. I had been up and down all night and was having a rough morning and I let it get to me.

While Glenn was out in the garage, I sat with Mama at the table and tearfully shared a little of my frustration. All my old insecurities came rushing up, and I wondered if everything was getting to him. "I don't know what is wrong with Glenn. I don't know why he won't talk to me. Do you think he's trying to find someone else?" It was a stupid thing to say, and I knew in my heart it wasn't true, but I had battled feelings of rejection all my life and was still training myself not to think that way.

I really didn't know how much Mama could understand and didn't really expect a response, so I was surprised when she gently said, "I don't think he's looking for someone."

It was elation I felt. My mother, my friend, reassuring me that what I feared was not true. In that one statement, I felt her concern, her wisdom, and encouragement to keep trying and have a little faith. I never expected so much. It was something we had missed in our relationship for so many years.

As it turned out, Glenn was just tired and stressed out about something at work that would pass and didn't want to talk about it with Mama there.

When I took Mama home, Papa would be waiting to help her into the house while I collected her things from the car. Then I would unpack and put everything away while Papa tended to Nanny. One day she was especially tired and so we went straight to the bedroom to change for bed. Papa was helping her take her shoes off and I was helping her with her sweater. She looked at both of us and said, "All this attention." We just laughed.

PAPA'S 70TH BIRTHDAY

The end of October 2009 would be Papa's 70th birthday. He deserved something special and it would be nice to have a gathering at the house again. He had been asking for some fried chicken. The problem was not knowing how Mama would do with so many people in the house. We decided to try a small dinner first and see how that went. So Susan and Bill came over for dinner one Sunday afternoon and we cooked and talked about it. Our little dinner went well, and we decided to go ahead and have a party. If Mama started getting nervous, I would go with her to her room and we would lie down. Or we could wind things up early. She really was pretty good about not getting upset with people around.

There were so many people that needed to come. They needed to see Mama and give Jackie encouragement – to let him know they were there if he needed them. We decided to invite everyone. We would have two waves. First wave would be dinner and cake for kids and grandkids, then later in the afternoon, cookies and coffee for Jackie's brothers and sisters, cousins, and friends and neighbors. I thought it would probably be the last big family gathering at the house.

We sent out invitations. Marty ordered a cake and Susan worked on cookies. Jack was taking care of the drinks and would be there to help us cook. I would dedicate myself to chicken and mashed potatoes.

It turned out to be a wonderfully sunny day. Almost all the family showed up for dinner. I fried more chicken than Colonel Sanders that day. I filled two skillets three times. I know that'll never happen again. As I cooked I greeted people when I got the chance, but there was one moment that captured my complete attention. When Susan and Bill's son, Sean and their daughter-in-law, Brandi came in carrying their new little bundle of joy, I stood holding my flour-coated fingers in front of me and watched. Their daughter, Caitie stood proudly beside Nanny as she quietly waited in her place at the table and watched Sean help Brandi unwrap the blanket. Then Brandi gently placed Paxton in Nanny's arms. What a precious gift.

As we gathered around Jackie at the kitchen table to sing Happy Birthday, I thought back to when Mama and Jackie

first got together. How it was just them and us five kids.
Now look what we've become! Most of the grandchildren are grown now holding children of their own, and
Marty's triplets, Walker, Layne, and Bryson, were
competing with the great-grandkids for a place at the table,
anticipating ice cream and cake and trying to get close to
their Papa. Our family overflowed into the living room
and out the sliding glass door and onto the deck as every
person in the house sang to Papa.

When the rest of the family and people Jackie worked with
and neighbors showed up there was no way everyone
could fit in the house. Reminiscent of a Sunday at Jackie's
parents' house, you had to turn sideways and scoot
through the doorways. Mama did great, but she did get
tired and started wringing her hands so I took her into her
room and we lay down on the bed and rested. We listened
to the familiar voices talking and laughing. After a few
minutes she said, "I feel sorry for him." I assumed she
meant Jackie. I took her hand in mine and held it close to
my heart and moved closer so my forehead would rest
against her shoulder.

SAYING GOODBYE

The first week in November 2009, I read an obituary for
my Aunt Bev.   I remembered hearing that she had breast
cancer. Mama was always the one to maintain the family
and friends connections. She kept us up to date, relating
marriages, changes in jobs, and illnesses. It was too late to
go to the funeral, but I wanted to visit the cemetery. If
you mentioned going somewhere, Mama would walk right

to the front door and want to go immediately, so I didn't say anything to Mama until Friday morning when we were getting ready to go to my house. I had picked a bouquet of roses, marigolds, purple cone flower, and blue salvia from my yard. They were the last blooms of the season. We tied a ribbon around them and went to say good-bye to Aunt Bev. The flowers on the grave were starting to wilt. We laid ours with the rest. I reminded Mama of the time when Aunt Bev came to live with us in Oklahoma when I had my broken leg and was unable to walk. I was glad to know, from the obituary, that she was a member of the Assembly of God church. It was comforting to hope that we would see her again.

So many wonderful women have gone. It won't be long until we too are gone from this earth to join them in heaven. Like the anticipation of childbirth, we gain courage to go through it knowing so many have gone before. It's a natural part of life. Everyone dies. We must be brave.

After we left the cemetery, we drove over to visit with my son, Austin. He was staying with his grandparents, his Dad's parents, George and Lavell. As we talked, Austin's dad, Allen, came in. They have a family plumbing business and they were getting ready to go to work. While we visited, I cut the obituary for Aunt Bev out of the newspaper. George told stories about back in the day, when his … "Mother canned everything she could get her hands on so they could make it through the winter during the depression. It wasn't easy canning on a wood stove in the summer heat with no air conditioning."

When we got ready to leave, Mama went right up to George and gave him a kiss on the cheek. I think it was her way of saying thank you. They have always been so good to us, helping us as much as they could. And then to my surprise, she gave Allen a kiss too. She had suffered with me through all the frustrations of our rocky relationship and then the heartbreak of divorce, but now it was time to let it go. All that was behind us now. I think that kiss said, "Thank you for being a loving and involved father to Austin and Aja."

CHRISTMAS

Our Christmas gatherings weren't always on Christmas Day. Many times, we would decide to get together on the Sunday after Christmas. It made it easier for the younger couples to make their plans, most of them making two and sometimes three stops in one day. In 2009, our gathering was set for Sunday afternoon at Marty's house. I was bringing homemade chicken noodle soup. Susan was bringing chili and chicken spaghetti. Jack was bringing devilled eggs and a veggie tray, and Marty was ordering Subway sandwiches.

We learned a long time ago to give Marty something easy to prepare. One year she was supposed to bake a ham. It was the main course. Everyone else was bringing sides and dessert. But for whatever reason, she didn't put the ham in the oven in time. When we got there, it had only been in the oven for half an hour. The solution? Jack cut slices and fried them in a skillet. Now that Marty has the triplets, she has the perfect excuse. We give her something easy to make.

In planning for our holiday, Mama spent the night with me on Saturday night that week, so we were bringing her with us to the Christmas gathering. I knew we might be a little late getting to Marty's, but I wanted to take Mama to church with us. It had been a long time since she had gone. I figured if she could sit in the waiting room at the doctor's office for an hour, she could sit through church, so we went. It was so nice to have her there. Everyone was glad to meet her. They had been praying for her - for us, for a long time.

 On the way to Marty's, I rode in the back seat and Glenn drove. Mama was in her usual spot in the passenger seat. It wasn't long before I noticed Mama starting to fidget. I realized she was getting too warm. I had Glenn stop the car so I could help her take her coat and scarf off. By the time she was buckled in again, the car was nice and cool. Sometimes you just do the best you can.

 Some of the grandkids hadn't seen Mama in a while. The changes in her appearance, her expressions, and her behavior showed an obvious decline. We were a little late getting there, and some were already eating.   After the welcoming hugs and the unloading of crackers, utensils, and soup, I noticed Jack's daughter, Sarah, brimming with tears, as she tried to choke down a sandwich. I knew she was devastated. It was her reality check. For me, it was the day of Mama's diagnosis, at the neurologist's office. I gave Sarah a hug and told her, "We all have those days. It's okay." Bless her heart. She just couldn't stop.

While Sarah cried, Mama ate. We gave her a bowl of chili

and a sandwich. After she ate that, she stood at the bar and nibbled at the sandwich fixings. So we gave her more. Then she nibbled some more. Susan, cornered me and asked, "Don't you think Mama's had enough?" I guess she didn't know when to quit anymore. We guided her to the living room where she could be entertained by her grandchildren and great-grandchildren.

THE NEW YEAR 2010

I remember Dad calling to wish me a Happy New Year. "Maybe next year will be better," he lied.

I responded, "Yeah, I don't know how it could be."

Sharon had spent a month in the hospital in October and then went back and forth for the next two months. Dad was ever by her side, telling his jokes and bribing the nurses to be nicer with pizza and flowers. Sharon wasn't doing well at all. She was on hospice now and was hardly eating anything at all. She was so weak she couldn't get out of bed by herself. I wanted to go see her so bad, but my finances were very limited. I was only working two days a week. And it was hard to think of leaving Mama.

Finally, one day when the roads were clear, I decided to take a day and just go. I knew if I didn't go now I wouldn't see Sharon again this side of heaven. I knew Dad would discourage me and I knew she didn't feel good and probably wouldn't look good, but I wanted to see her while she lived. So I didn't call, I just got up early and left. After six hours of driving I pulled in the driveway, called Dad from there and asked him if he wanted to have a cup of hot tea and visit a little.

He said, "Why? Are you going to mail me some?"

"Nope, I'm here. In your driveway!" It was so good to see him. I was worried about him. He was losing Sharon, and he was taking care of her all by himself. I wanted to be sure Dad was taking care of himself. I wanted to know that he was doing alright.

I checked to see that he had good food in the refrigerator. There were lots of Ziploc bags of snacks in the kitchen, like cheese puffs and candy. I asked him about it and he showed me the ice cream in the freezer. He said, "When Sharon gets a craving, I go to the store. That's all she will eat."

We talked about how he was doing and then I sat with Sharon while she ate some cheese puffs and we watched General Hospital. It had been so long since I had watched the soap I had forgotten the names of all the characters. She had to refresh my memory. I filled her water cup while I was there, and encouraged her to drink more water, realizing she wasn't worried about how much water she drank anymore, but hoping she would understand it was just me trying to say I care. I couldn't stay long. I had to drive back home the same day, but I was glad for the chance to say good-bye. It was a sad time, but I wanted to see Sharon. I wanted her to know I loved her, to talk to her, to kiss her, to say good-bye.

GETTING SOME HELP

In January, we applied for Medicaid. We had heard of a program that would pay someone to help Mama with personal care. And they would let the family choose who they wanted to be the caregiver and it could even be a member of the family. I was the one for the job. She needed someone and if I was going to spend so much time helping that I couldn't work, I would need to get paid something, at least enough to cover the expense of gas.

All of our lives, we heard Mama and Jackie talk about how people shouldn't take from the government; that people should work for a living if they can and support themselves and their families. And they did that. They worked hard all their lives, but there was never enough to save for retirement. So now, they were relying on Social Security, Medicaid, and Medicare. They paid in all their lives, and they needed it now.

We weighed our options. We didn't want to put Mama in a nursing home, but if we did, the Social Security check wouldn't be enough to cover it, so they would rely on Medicaid to meet the remainder of the cost of her care. I understand it can be expensive for someone to be cared for in a nursing home, sometimes over $3000 a month.

In comparison, the program we were applying for would pay me $600 a month, then raise it up to $1200 a month a few months down the road when Mama would require more hours of care, a better deal for everyone all the way around. I wasn't sure if they would require me to work through an agency and didn't know if they would expect me to have training, but thought it would be good to have some training, so I applied at Area Agency on Aging, thinking I might be able to help someone else in addition to helping Mama.

They put me in a two week class where we learned about standards of care, how to make the house safer, how to give personal care, and how to take blood pressure. We learned how to lift and move patients and how to operate equipment and what to expect as dementia runs its course. We watched a movie called *Grace* about a woman who had Alzheimer's disease and her precious husband who took care of her. It was very enlightening and very touching.

It turned out that there was no training required for me to be the caregiver through the program we were applying for. And it turned out that I didn't have any extra time to help anyone else, but having gone through the training gave me a little confidence and some practical knowledge that I put to good use.

It was very hard on Jackie to handle things on his own for the two weeks while I was in class. His brother Jerry's wife, Carol, came to sit with Mama one day so Jackie could run errands. Carol was always a good friend to Mama. They always enjoyed visiting. But this was different. Jackie and I worried about what we would do if something happened to one of us. We just prayed we would have the strength to see this through.

After the class, we talked about ways to make things safer. We picked up the throw rugs everywhere but the bathroom and we got a nice bathmat for the tub.

It took a couple of months for the Medicaid application to process. And then I had to wait for the payroll cycle to be completed before I could get paid. My pocketbook was stretched so thin I could see through it.

REGRET

At the end of February, Sharon passed away. She was at the hospital for the last few weeks. Dad only left her side to go home for a shower and to eat. He was getting very little sleep. I was amazed at his dedication and strength. Sharon, bravely, donated her body to science hoping to help find a cure for cancer. They would keep her remains for up to two years. I hurt for Daddy. And he was so far away.

Sharon's death upset me more than I expected. I thought that since I had never lived with her, since we lived so far apart, and since our conversations were few and far between that I would be spared some level of grief. What I didn't realize was the great loss I would feel. I regretted not cultivating our relationship.

In September, before I knew Sharon was sick, I had decided to call more often. Knowing Mama was soon to leave this world, I hoped we might develop a closer relationship. Not that she could ever replace Mama, just like I could never replace Sharon's daughter, Stacy who died from cancer in 2002.

I remember a visit to Dad and Sharon's house ten years ago. She had been going through her closet and was ready to get rid of some things. She gave me eight or ten broomstick skirts with matching sweaters. I loved them. They were so comfortable and easy to take care of.

She loved to shop. One day when they were visiting me, we went to the mall. I needed a couple of bras and was looking at the usual department stores, but she guided me to Victoria's Secret. She showed me a plain bra of modest design with an underwire for support and said, "Try this one. This is all I wear."

It was nice to have her watching out for me.

In 2000, I was recently divorced, and had lost my job. I was pretty down. I was struggling with issues of rejection. Dad felt so bad for me he decided to do something he had wanted to do for a long, long time. He hired an attorney and they drew up adoption papers. Sharon agreed happily.

I told Dad, I would be okay; he didn't have to go through with it. He would always be my Daddy. But he said, "No, I really want to do this." Maybe he regretted that he hadn't done it when I was a child. I was an infant when he married Mama and they had always talked about "getting my name changed" but money was always short and we were busy with life.

So I went to Oklahoma City to sign the papers at the courthouse and it was official. At the age of 40, I had a new name and a new sense of belonging. It was reassuring to know he wanted and loved me enough to go to all that trouble. He always tells people that after the judge signed the papers he shook Dad's hand and said, "Congratulations, it's a girl."

SORROW

After Sharon died, I found it was too much of an effort to go to church. I was tired. I was at Mama's Monday through Wednesday, was off on Thursday and then I had her with me at my house on Friday and Saturday which left me exhausted. And there was another reason I didn't go. The sorrow of what we were going through was too great. And with Sharon's death added to it, I felt like I was too sad to be around people. I didn't want to drag them down and I was too tired to smile. I put on my happy face every day when I would walk in the door at Mama's and I just didn't have any left for Sunday.

Now I know it's not supposed to be that way. We are supposed to give our burden to the Lord and let other people help us and support us emotionally, but sometimes it takes time. When someone you love is slowly dying, you mourn for every lost function. You give up one thing at a time. Can't make the bed anymore, can't brush her teeth anymore, can't get her own food, can't talk, can't dress herself. So we try to make the best of things.

My sweet friends at church had been praying and were genuinely concerned, and I appreciated them so much, but I just couldn't go.

LOSING YOUR MARBLES AND OTHER SAYINGS

Funny how we say things without a second thought when

all is as it should be. Now when those sayings come to mind, I find myself looking for a kinder way to say things. I remember at Jackie's birthday party, one of our visitors was telling me a story about remodeling being done at her church and as she got to the end of the story, I knew what she was going to say, because she hesitated after, "bats in …"

So I finished for her, "bats in the belfry?" It was just a polite moment of hesitation as she realized it may not be the time and place for such a phrase. There are so many things we say. We call each other silly goose, refer to each other as lost as a goose, say we are losing our marbles or losing our minds.

One day Jackie's brother Charlie was talking about his mother-in-law. He and Phyllis had recently moved her mother to the nursing home. Charlie was empathizing with Jackie, "It just doesn't seem right. We went up to the nursing home to see Phyllis's mother and the poor woman doesn't know if she's washing or hanging out! What's the Lord thinking?"

Mama enjoyed sneaking up behind Jackie when he wasn't expecting it. Jackie would call her his little Comanche or accuse her of being one of Geronimo's girls when she would startle him. She thought that was pretty funny. As Mama got worse, she found many things amusing that were previously off limits. We still didn't say the F word, but we laughed when it happened. One day I sat on the edge of the bathtub as Mama was doing her business. You had to stay with her in case she forgot and got up in the middle of something. And she needed help with her pants. When there was an unexpected noise, I turned quickly and looked behind the shower curtain and said loudly, "Hey you! Be quiet in there, no pootin' in there!" Then she laughed and laughed. Laughter is good.

OBSESSIVE COMPULSIVE

There was a period of a few months when Mama would go in the bathroom and flush the toilet over and over. I had to follow her around to make sure she didn't go in there and flush it. Glenn said, "She's going to flood the septic tank." At home, Jackie put duct tape on the handle and told her it was broken. She just moved the tape and flushed it anyway. Sometimes she would do it two or three times in a half hour. I finally turned the water off on the toilet at my house. She would also turn on the light in the bathroom and sometimes I would find the heater running, so Glenn installed a cover on the switch for the heater.

As Mama became nervous and anxious, she picked at the threads in her fuchsia robe until she made a bare spot. She used the robe to cover up with when she laid on her couch. One day I noticed she had a safety pin with a bead on it pinned to the robe's tag. She would spin the bead and move it around, sliding it from one end of the pin to the other. At my house, I gave her a thimble to carry. It was a familiar object. I hoped it would be a comfort to her, something to fiddle with, to occupy her. She would put it on her finger and carry it with her everywhere. She even slept with it.

She was also obsessive about her eating. She didn't know

when to quit. She ate three oranges in one afternoon at my house and wanted more. She wanted to eat everything. One day, I had the dog treats sitting on the kitchen counter and had given one to my lab, Lucy. Mama started to open the package. I asked her if she wanted to give Lucy a treat. She kept trying to open it, so I helped her get it open. She took out a Canine Carry Out and I told her to give it to Lucy, but she started to put it into her mouth. I thought she was kidding, but she wasn't. I had to keep the dog treats put away after that, and anything else that could be mistaken for food. That reminds me; she was always letting the dog and cat in and out. It wasn't so bad if the weather was nice, but when it was cold, having the door open so much was a problem.

It was around this time that she would pick up anyone's glass and drink out of it. She didn't care. But now that she wasn't supposed to have sugar, I had to watch her. I had to hide my drink and keep hers in sight.

She was continually adjusting the blinds, raising and lowering, opening and closing and at her house arranging the curtains and straightening the cover on Jackie's chair in the living room. The urge to straighten it was so strong that if Jackie was sitting in it, she would stand in front of the chair until he would get up and let her straighten it. Then he would sit back down. Why not let her?

When I took her home on Saturdays, I would tell Jackie what we had for dinner, how she helped me fold the clothes, and what made her smile. He would sit in his chair by the window and she would stand beside him, in her favorite sweater, looking out the window. Week after week, I watched them there. A little tremor would shake her hand and he would reach out to hold it still for her. As the conversation continued, they would continue to hold each other's hands and Papa would say the things that would make her smile and sometimes we would laugh and she would look at him and move her mouth like she wanted to say something. Jackie would say, "Talk to Papa," but nothing would come out.

THE PARK

In the spring, we started taking walks in the city park. The park is located only a few blocks from their house. There is a small lake with a walking trail that meanders all the way around. I would help her out of the car and if she had a pocket, I would tell her to hold onto the keys for me. As we walked, I would have to remind her not to put her hands in her pockets in case she stumbled, so her hands would be free to help catch her. She liked her pockets. She liked to look at the ducks and the geese, but she didn't want to feed them. We would walk down to the bench that was at the edge of the golf course. Then we would sit and rest and gaze across the water rippling in the breeze. If we were lucky, the sunshine would make sparkles dance on the water. Once in a while we would hear the familiar sound of a golf cart whizzing on the path or the knock of a club hitting a golf ball. We listened to the chatter of the geese and the splash of their wings on the water. And we enjoyed the dark green of the cedars against the blue, blue sky.

A few times, we walked the other direction. There was a

bench on that side too, but you had to walk up a steep little hill to get to it. Then as summer approached, they moved a little building with a porch on it to the edge of the lake to serve as an office for renting paddle boats. It was never open when we were walking, so we would sit on the little porch and rest. One day, as we stood beside the building, I noticed she was looking at a sign taped to the window of the building. I moved closer to the sign and asked her if she could still read some words. She stepped close enough to touch the sign and pointed to the bottom word, "THANKS!"

I said it, "Thanks? You know that word?" And then it hit me. *Was she trying to tell me something?* I said, "Are you telling me thank you?"

She blinked.

I'll take that as a yes, I thought with a smile.

On the way back to the car, I would guide her as we maneuvered around the duck droppings on the sidewalk. We usually walked three or four times a week. We kept it up all through the summer, but had to stop in September, when she started slowing down and falling.

Papa would take her for walks at home on Sundays. They would walk down the driveway and up the slope to the street that ran along the side of the house. They would continue down to the end of the block to the stop sign and come back. One cloudy day, they got caught in a rain shower. They hurried to get back to the house and instead of going all the way down to the corner and coming up the driveway, Mama decided to take a shortcut down the grassy slope from the road heading straight for the carport. When her foot hit the wet grass on the slope, she slid down on her bottom. She wasn't hurt. She looked up at Jackie with a grin. They had a good laugh in the rain and somehow he managed to help her up. He said he put her hands around the back of his neck and pulled her up. I told him he better not hurt himself; I couldn't make it without my partner!

VISITS FROM THE BOYS

Marty started bringing the boys by more often since the weather was nice and they could play outside. Sometimes she would call and ask if we had eaten lunch yet and would bring pizza or burgers and fries. She always had something for the boys to eat (like cupcakes!) and she brought extra for us. The boys were always happy to see their Papa and Nanny. They would fight over which one would wear Papa's cowboy hat and they would go out in the backyard to take turns sitting on Papa's mower. One day as Walker sat on Papa's lap, he looked up at his balding head and said, "Where's Papa's hair?" It took a minute for us to register what he said. Papa said, "What?" Walker repeated, "Where's Papa's hair?" It sank in that time. "Oh! Papa lost it, you ornery little toot!"

EATING ON A SCHEDULE

Every morning, unless there was a doctor's appointment that required fasting, Jackie would fix breakfast. They had oatmeal or Cream of Wheat with toast, or scrambled eggs

118

with bacon, and sometimes he would even make sausage with biscuits and gravy. I would come in about the time they were finishing breakfast and help her shower and get dressed. Then we would walk. After that, it would be time for a snack. Sometimes I would take her to get a milkshake. Most of the time she would have a peanut butter and jelly sandwich with milk. Then she would lie down for a while. I would do a few things around the house and then it would be time for lunch. You could ask her if she was ready to have something to eat and sometimes she would say, "Yeah, okay." Sometimes just, "Yeah." But rarely, did she say, "No." Usually, she would just go in the kitchen and sit in her chair when she wanted to eat.

At times, she would get antsy while in the middle of a meal and want to get up from the table. I started taking her to the bathroom before meals just to be sure she didn't need to go, but she would get up anyway, sometimes three or four times in just a few minutes. In the afternoon she usually had cottage cheese with fruit for her snack. After that it would be time for me to wind things up and head for my house. Jackie would have their dinner ready around five o'clock in the evening. Then before bed she and Jackie would have a little cup of pudding or applesauce or yogurt. After their bedtime snack, Jackie would let her throw away the empty containers until he realized he was losing spoons in the trash.

She was still pretty good about feeding herself, but she was getting messy and the bites she was taking were way too big. My daughter, Aja, made a beautiful apron for me for Mother's Day. When it was time to fix something for

Mama to eat I decided I would put on my apron and put an apron on Mama too. Then when it was time to eat she would already have her apron on and it would keep her from messing up her clothes. It worked for a little while, but it wasn't long before she started having trouble getting the spoon or fork to her mouth. She would lift the fork about six inches off the plate and then stop like she couldn't go any higher, so I would guide it to her mouth. But she could still eat a peanut butter sandwich with her left hand. When Jackie and I started feeding her, she didn't need an apron anymore.

NEW GLASSES

We had been putting off her eye exam. Her glasses were a little scratched, but seemed to be working alright. I remember pointing out a squirrel in the tree in the front yard and watching her follow it with her eyes. I knew she could see it, but there was no way to tell if it was clear to her. She was taking her glasses off and laying them down. We weren't sure if they needed adjustment or if the prescription needed to be updated. Finally, one day at my house, she laid her glasses on the bed and sat on them. The earpiece broke off.

The exam went well. She was able to cooperate and follow instructions and the doctor was able to tell what she needed without much input. We narrowed the frames down to three that looked like what she would wear and told her to pick. She picked up a pair. "Those are the ones I would have picked!" I exclaimed. She was proud of her new glasses, but she was never as comfortable with them as the old ones.

WEARING THIN

By June, the afternoon crying, pacing, and screaming was just too much to bear. While I was there, Jackie got out of the house as much as he could, even if it was just mowing or working in the yard. And I took Mama out as much as I dared. She would control herself better if we were out. But it was the afternoons that were hard. She would sit at the table and hit it with the palm of her hand. We would grab her hand and hold it, telling her not to do that, she was going to hurt herself. It was wearing on Mama too. We decided to go back to the doctor and determined to try some kind of medication. We needed something to calm her down when she started getting upset. We wanted something tried and true, something that had been widely used so that we would know what kind of side effects to expect. Her neurologist was so busy it was going to take longer than a month to get in to see her so Mama's primary care physician recommended us to a different neurologist. Even so, the appointment was a couple of weeks away so the doctor gave us a prescription for Xanax as a temporary solution until we could get in to see the neurologist. The Xanax helped a little and even that little was a great relief. But we knew it wasn't a long term solution.

When we went to see the new neurologist, we told him about the tremors. He explained that it was part of the disease progression. We asked if she could be in pain. He observed she didn't have the characteristics of a person in pain, such as a set jaw, pale complexion, lips stretched tight, sweating, or moaning. It made sense to us. We told him about the agitation and screaming. He prescribed Risperidal. It is an antipsychotic. It worked! We split the tablets and gave her a half three times a day. As long as we did that, it kept her agitation to a minimum. After a few weeks, it sunk in that it really was helping. Jackie joked, "Lord, you finally did something good for this girl."

Looking back, maybe it would have been better if we had pushed to find the right medication sooner. It was a fear of doing more damage that made us wait until we couldn't take it anymore. We waited until we could see that it was wearing her out. Of course, we knew the disease was taking a toll too and we didn't know how much to attribute to her being upset so much of the time. Some medications have terrible side effects, such as tremors, lip smacking, and uncontrolled tongue movement. I remembered people I had seen in the nursing homes and wondered how much of their unusual movements were a side effect of drugs. We had already experienced the side effect of tremors and that was the start of Mama's crying and screaming episodes. Maybe she would be susceptible to more side effects. Some of the medications even warned of possible sudden death when used by elderly patients with dementia. So we waited, not wanting to put her through the trauma of side effects and not wanting to lose her.

FACEBOOK

At my house, when she would lie down to rest, I would sit

at my computer and look at pictures of my kids, my sisters, and my nieces and nephews. If she was awake, I would turn the computer so she could see the newest cutest pictures. She liked it. Soon, she would sit down in my chair at the computer and wait for me to pull up a chair and open Facebook. I'd say, "Who do we want to visit today?" "How's my nephew Dillon doing? Doesn't he look nice dressed for the prom?" "Let's see if newlyweds Anthony and Cassie have posted any pictures of their new house." "Look at Leanne's, little girls, how big they are getting! And so pretty."   And we would see what Susan was saying and look at Aja's pictures on her blog. She was enjoying it so much that I made a Facebook account for her and uploaded a few pictures. It was fun for a while, but after a few weeks I started hearing her sigh. We would look at a few things and then she would get a melancholy look and sigh. I said, "I know Mama, I miss them too. They're busy with their lives like we were not long ago." And I decided to take her visiting.

First, we went to see Susan. It wasn't much further than my house. Susan was home with her grandson Paxton. We were so happy to hold little Pax. He was so full of energy and bright as a button. His little eyes followed Susan around the room as we held him so gently.

MAYCEE BELLE

Then we went to a baby shower at Susan's church. Susan's daughter, my niece, Aimee was going to have a girl. We wrapped up the pink and taupe rug we had crocheted and off we went. It was great to see Aimee so beautifully pregnant and a treat to have cake and ice cream.

While we were at the shower, we talked to Aunt Reba Jo and promised to come by for a visit. In a week or so, we dropped by. While we were there, Aunt Reba Jo showed us Uncle Troy's favorite family pictures. We stayed so long, we missed Mama's mid-morning snack. As we were leaving, Reba Jo told me, "I'm sorry this is happening to your mother."

I forgot to tell her about finding Uncle Troy's toothpick while cleaning the top of Mama's refrigerator. Just like Grandpa, you would often see Uncle Troy with a toothpick in his mouth. I guess he laid one down at Mama's and she kept it. It was in a little Ziploc bag labeled in Mama's handwriting, "Troy's toothpick."

In June when Maycee Belle was born, Grandpa John came to town to see her. We had lunch with Susan and Bill and their family and then went to the hospital to see the new baby. I wished Mama and Jackie could have been there. We set aside the sadness for a moment.

After Aimee took her wee one home, we gave her a couple of days to settle in and then I took Mama and Jackie to see Maycee Belle. Mama was captivated. She couldn't take her eyes off her precious great-granddaughter. We all took turns holding her. Mama held her too, although she seemed a little awkward as if she wasn't quite comfortable. We stayed right beside her so we could take Maycee Belle if Mama got tired. While I was there Maycee Belle's big sisters, Kalynn and Baleigh, showed me the baby's room. They pointed out all the new furniture and bedding and showed me all of Maycee Belle's dresses. She was going to be the best dressed girl in town for months to come.

THE GARDEN

In June, the row of blackberries behind the garden at my house began to produce. Every three or four days I would pick a large bowl full. Mama loved to be outside. I would put my straw hat on her and grab the big bowl. She didn't know which ones to pick, so I was the picker and she was the bowl holder. Our blackberries are thornless, so that makes the picking easier. She would follow me as I worked my way up one side and down the other. She stayed close to me as I knelt, looking up from the bottom and moving the leaves aside, not wanting to miss any of the juicy, sweet berries. Sometimes, I would find an extra plump berry and would ask her if she wanted it. She usually didn't respond, but I would pop it into her mouth. She loved them. As I maneuvered to place my handfuls of berries into the bowl I realized she was feasting on blackberries. "You like them like that? I guess that's what they're for," I laughed.

There were many trips to the garden to harvest radishes, peppers, tomatoes, cucumbers, and squash. Many times she would hold the bucket while I cut the okra. There were times when we were cooking that I would take her with me to pull an onion, or cut some rosemary, or basil. When the corn was ready, she watched me break off the ears, pile them up, and tromp down the stalks. Then we sat on the back porch and she helped me pull the husks off the sticky golden rows of sunshine.

Most days, we would take a walk around the yard to see what was blooming. Some days twice. We would walk down the driveway to the front of the yard where in the spring, daffodils, phlox, and tulips put on a show in front of an old rock wall. That wall has marked the edge of a pasture for as long as anyone can remember. Later there were irises, and crepe myrtle. Bees and butterflies entertained us. Clematis, echinacea, and marigolds occupied our minds. We snipped a rose to carry with us to the picnic table where we sat gazing across the pastures, soaking up the sunshine, amused at my lab Lucy rolling on her back in the grass under the trees and the blue, blue sky.

I let Mama take the lead from there. There were so many decisions she couldn't make anymore. Which direction to walk next was something she could handle. I was surprised when she began to weave through the low hanging branches of the elms that surround our picnic table. She was like a child, playfully weaving through the uneven limbs.

FALLING DOWN

As the disease progressed, Mama was more likely to stumble. Walking used to come natural, but now it required her full attention. One day at her house, she missed her step as she was going up the front porch steps. She grabbed the post and hung on as she slid to the ground. Papa helped her up, but she was afraid to go up the stairs. Soon, Papa got busy building a ramp for the front porch with the help of their neighbors, Scott and Tammy. My brother, Steve, worked on a ramp for the deck in the back. At my house, Glenn framed lattice for rails around both porches. As I visited with other people who have cared for a loved one with dementia at home, I realized how common it is for people to build ramps, rails, enclosures, gates, and even fences to keep their family members safe.

Nurses came each month to see if we had the supplies we needed and to see how Mama was doing. They kept asking, "Is she falling yet?" After three months of the same question we got the feeling that when she did start falling it must signal the end getting closer. It wasn't long before she missed her chair in the kitchen and landed on the floor. Thankfully, nothing was broken. Mama was young to have dementia, only in her mid-sixties, and she was strong. We tried not to let her out of our sight, so we could intervene if she was nearing a rough spot.

She started having problems getting into bed. Her bed was tall enough that you couldn't sit down on it and roll back. You had to climb up with your knee to get in it. One morning, Jackie found her in the floor on the other side of the bed. She wasn't able to get up by herself. There was no way to know how long she had been waiting for someone to help her. We decided we would have to put away her old bed. We moved it to the spare bedroom and got a frame to put the mattress and foundation on so it would be lower, easier to get into, and not as far to fall from. Still she had trouble getting into bed. She would forget and try to get into the bed the old way, with her knee first. She wouldn't get far enough up on the bed and her bottom would roll off the edge and she would land on the floor. It had to be hard on her back, but she never showed any signs of a problem from it.

It happened at my house too. She tried to get into the bed, knee first and slid off the edge. When she started to fall she grabbed the scarf on the dresser next to the bed and pulled the lamp and everything else off on her head. I was only a few steps behind her, but not close enough to stop her. There she was sitting on her bottom with the lampshade on her head, glasses hanging off one ear, holding the lamp in her hands. "Ohhh, Mama. Are you okay?"

One day as we headed for the car to take Mama home, she stumbled and fell on the sidewalk. Her reflexes were so diminished that she couldn't catch herself. She landed on her chest, trying to hold her head up, but still bruising her cheek. I was so angry with myself for letting her walk alone. For a few days, I doubted whether I should be doing this. My sweet sisters encouraged me to keep going. We were in a battle. It was a balance between freedom and restraint.

After Jackie woke up one morning and found Mama sitting in the floor in the utility room, we decided to block off the end of the hallway at night. If she got up at night she would only be able to go to the bathroom or Jackie's room. It was getting harder for her to get out of bed by herself. Maybe that was a good thing. We hated to see her decline, but at least we wouldn't have to worry about her falling if she couldn't get up by herself.

SPENDING TIME IN THE BATHROOM

Let's back up a little. As Mama forgot how to do things, I began to learn how she wanted things done. We bought a hand shower so I could help Mama rinse her hair. She had trouble getting all the shampoo out of her hair, so I started helping her. When I put the shampoo on, I took the opportunity to massage her scalp. She loved it. She loved her hot shower. I gave her one almost every day. After turning the water off, I put a small towel on her hair to catch the drips and wrapped her big towel around her arms from the front for modesty and to keep her warm while I helped her out of the tub. I tried to be gentle as I dried her, keeping her covered as much as possible. I massaged her scalp again with the little towel as I dried her hair.

As it became more difficult for her to get in and out of the tub I would have her lean forward on me as I lifted her knee to get her foot over the side. Then I would let go of her leg and support her by resting her arms in mine with my hands near her elbows. Holding her as she stepped down and backing up with her so she could pull her other leg over.

Mama spent a lot of time in the bathroom. She would stand in front of the sink when she wanted her teeth brushed. And she liked to look at herself in the mirror. I think she liked to see that familiar face, kind of like an old friend. Jackie would be busy around the house and realize he hadn't seen her in a few minutes and would go looking for her in the bathroom. Sometimes she would be standing in front of the bathroom window gazing out to the backyard. One day, he found her standing at the bathroom window in front of the toilet in her housedress peeing all over the floor. When he told me his story, he said it, "sounded like a cow peein' on a big rock."

None of this appeared to bother Mama, so we would laugh and rib each other, "Glad it was you and not me."

At first, this is something you dread - the toileting problems, but really, it was a breeze compared to the emotional part. It was just something to clean up and actually, something to make a big deal about. We would get happy when she made it to the potty. With a child, you are teaching and training, knowing there will be improvement. When you are helping someone with dementia, you have to remember they are not learning, they are forgetting, so you just do the best you can. When she was walking by herself, she would go to the bathroom over and over and over, sometimes three or four times in fifteen minutes.

I'd say, "Mama, we just went to the bathroom."

Jackie would say, "Mama, your butt didn't stay on the couch long enough for it to get warm." Or, "You weren't on the couch long enough for your butt to leave a print."

We learned not to scold or be disappointed when there was an accident. In fact, we made such a to-do over the successes, that, at times I think she thought *we* were the ones losing our marbles. There were times when we went through four or five outfits a day. It happened even though we were using pads. She couldn't tell she needed to go until it started happening and then we would head for the bathroom and in the process of getting the pants down and getting situated, the back of the pants would get wet.

Most of the accidents happened in the late afternoon and evening. She would drink water all day and by evening she was overflowing. We soon learned to limit her water after dinner to keep the cleanup to a minimum at night. Sleep is important for everyone. We put a spray bottle of disinfectant and paper towels under the sink in the bathroom. (Pine Sol diluted with water works well and goes a long way.) The goal was to keep the slippers and socks dry, if you could. So we wiped up the puddles and changed the clothes and we were ready to go another round. Papa did laundry almost every day for months.

One day, Papa told me a story about getting her cleaned up after an accident in the bathroom. He had changed her pants, but that was all. Then as he passed by her on the couch he noticed she was taking off her socks. She looked up at him and said, "Wet." It was always a thrill to us for her to use a different word or to say anything at all. It was a peek into her mind. It let us know what she was capable of thinking.

Don't get me wrong, we did get tired. I remember one night at my house, after a long, trying day, I lay down on the cot by her bed thinking she was asleep, and as soon as I dozed off, I heard the bed creak. Off we went to the bathroom. And nothing. It hadn't been long enough for her to have to go, but I guess she wanted to make sure. So we waltzed back to the bed and dozed off again. Then I heard the bed creak again. I knew it hadn't been more than ten minutes. I thought, *I don't know if I can take much more of this*. So we danced our way to the potty again.

On the way back from our fourth trip to the bathroom in an hour, I broke. I burst into tears and looked up at the ceiling and said, "Lord, just take me now. I can't do this anymore!" Mama just laughed. She laughed out loud. So I began to laugh and we went to bed and slept for a few hours.

When Dad was visiting in June, he unloaded some things he thought Mama might be able to use. There was a bedside potty chair that he said Sharon never used, blue square plastic-backed pads for the beds, some disposable briefs, some giant disposable diapers, and some two foot square quilts with water resistant backing that were washable. We knew it was just a matter of time until we would need protection for the mattresses.

In August, we switched to bigger pads at night, and then started using them all the time. We bought rubber mattress covers and put the blue pads under the sheets. When she started having accidents at night, Papa went to the thrift stores and bought extra sheets. Susan talked us into trying pull-ups at night. We loved them so much we used them in the daytime too. Still sometimes the pull-ups would leak at night. Instead of Jackie changing the bed in the middle of the night, he would change her pull-up and her clothes and then spread one of the little quilts Dad had brought under her to keep her dry until morning.

We really tried to help her maintain her dignity as long as we could and maybe longer than we should have in this case. She didn't mind the pull-ups at all.

MORE VISITING

One sunny morning, I took Mama to see her brother Joe. I had heard he was having some health problems and that his daughter Tanny was helping him. The day we visited, she wasn't there, but Uncle Joe was glad to see us. He welcomed us in and I told him a little about what we were up against. He helped Mama get comfortable by giving her a pillow to put behind her back in the big recliner. We talked a little about the weather, his health, gardens, and heaven.

On the way out, he walked Mama to the car while I put the watermelon he gave us in the back. Then I went around to help her get in the car. I stood by them while he took her hands in his and looked into her eyes for a long moment. He told her he loved her. They didn't seem to notice me there. I wondered if they sailed back in time together. They just smiled at each other. Then he said, "Does this look like home to you?"

When life gets hard, isn't that what we all want. To be home again where things are safe and right, like it was when we were kids?

In August, my daughter Aja had to have emergency surgery for endometriosis. She was very weak and in a lot of pain from cysts that were leaking blood and fluid into her abdomen. Her doctor said it was the worst case she had ever seen. For days after the surgery, Aja was too nauseated to eat. It took a while for her to recover. After Aja was home for a couple of days, Nanny and Papa went with me to visit our sweet girl. She was doing well, getting better every day. Her husband, Mike was taking good care of her. While we were there, he was preparing her lunch, so since it was time for Nanny's snack he made some for her too. In no time, he had put together a spinach salad and warmed a bowl of delicious chicken soup his step-mother Mary had brought. While Aja ate, I fed Mama. It had been a while since they had enjoyed a meal together.

ENCOURAGEMENT

On her bad days, I told Mama, "Maybe Jesus will come soon. And we will be changed, in a moment, in the twinkling of an eye, together. And we won't have to die."

I wondered if she would enjoy hearing familiar scriptures, hoping that they would bring comfort and encouragement, ease her fears, and strengthen her faith. I got out her Bible and began reading from II Timothy, "God has not given us a spirit of fear, but of power, and love and of a sound mind."

She said, "It doesn't make sense."

But when we talked about heaven, it made sense to her. I would quote John 14 and she would nod and blink.

> "Let not your heart be troubled, you believe in God, believe also in me. In my Father's house are many mansions; if it were not so, I would have told you. I go to prepare a place for you. And if I go and prepare a place for you, I will come again and receive you unto myself; that where I am, there you may be also. And

134

where I go you know, and the way you know."

John 14:1-4

As we drove to my house one Friday, she seemed especially sad. We usually listened to the radio, but this day it was quiet. As I searched for the right words to comfort her, the tune to an old hymn rose out of my heart. As I sang, she nodded and agreed with her eyes.

> Farther along we'll know all about it.
> Farther along we'll understand why.
> Cheer up my brother, live in the sunlight.
> We'll understand it all by and by.

HURRY UP AND CLEAN UP

One advantage to having Mama at my house was that I could clean. It seemed like if I sat down, she would get up. The moment I tried to take a break, she would need something. So I stayed busy. There was plenty to do and as long as I was cleaning, she would stay with me. It seemed to satisfy her. She couldn't do it, but she had a way of telling me what needed to be done, such as running her finger through the dust on the bookshelf in the living room or pointing out the cleanser smudge that I missed on the shower door.

It was becoming more difficult to find time for myself. For a long time, I would fix Mama something to eat and leave her at the table with Glenn on guard to make sure she didn't try to go outside while I took a shower. Then I would shower as quickly as I could. A friend from work who had cared for an elderly parent gave Glenn a DVD of the Three Stooges. Sometimes Glenn would play the DVD to entertain Mama while I dressed. She would stand in front of the TV and chuckle at their antics.

After she began falling while getting into bed, I was afraid to let her out of my sight. I decided it would be better to give up a little privacy to keep her safe, so when it was time for me to get cleaned up, I would take her in the bedroom and shut the door behind us. When I was ready to get in the shower, I would close the lid to the potty and have her sit on it. I told her I needed her to help me so I could get ready and I wanted her to stay right there so she would be safe while I showered. I would peek out and make sure she was still there. She would stay right there until I was done every time.

Jackie would wait until I was there to take his shower, and it was a challenge to shave or even go to the bathroom when he was alone with her.

THE EVENING ROUTINE

When we were at my house, I tried to follow the routine that worked for Jackie at home. Mama was ready for dinner by five or five-thirty. After dinner I would brush her teeth and straighten up the kitchen. By that time, she would be ready to change for bed. I would help her dress and turn down the bed. She was often nervous at this time of the day and would go to the doors and open them. We locked the doors and tried to distract her.

I thought music might hold her attention, so we went to

her room and I pulled up YouTube and found some of the entertainers she used to listen to when I was a child: Barbara Streisand, Frank Sinatra, Dean Martin, and others. She would look at the screen for a minute and start with her pacing again. I searched for the Bill Gaither Trio and played the inspirational favorite, "Because He Lives." She sat down in the chair right in front of my computer and watched the whole song. Amazingly, she sat there for half an hour while I played more of The Gaithers.

She would want to lie down, so I would help her into bed, but she wouldn't stay put for long. She would be back and forth to the bathroom. By seven o'clock, she would be hungry again. I would ask her if she wanted a snack and she would sit on the couch with us and watch Funniest Home Videos and eat yogurt, pudding, or applesauce. She always got a laugh out of the silly videos.

She started having problems taking her pills at night, so we crushed them and gave them to her in the first bite of her bedtime snack. At bedtime, she took her little half (the Risperidal) and a Benadryl to help her sleep. We had started the Benadryl in June. Then I would tuck her in and give her three kisses. That's what Papa said she needed. And I would sit with Glenn and watch TV for an hour or so. Sometimes she would stay in bed, sometimes she would be up and down, but after a little while, I was so tired, I would go lie down in her room on the cot Glenn's mom had given us. From there I could hear the bed creak if she tried to get up and I could help her so she wouldn't fall. She usually woke up every couple of hours, but we managed to get a little sleep.

The Hardest Part

The Last Six Months

FOOD PROCESSING

She started holding things in her mouth. Jackie would tell me how when he brushed her teeth at night she would still have pieces of dinner in her cheek. And we discovered her holding her pills in her mouth. They would be half dissolved when she would take them out and hand them to us. That had to taste terrible. She started picking the fruit out of her yogurt. I would give her a bite of oatmeal and the raisins would come back out. She wasn't chewing her food like she should, so we started chopping her food.

It was getting harder to prepare meals and keep an eye on Mama at the same time. She wouldn't sit still for any length of time, and we were afraid she would fall. More than once, Jackie would get something started for dinner and would have to turn it all off to help Mama in the bathroom. We were tired and rushed but wanted to have healthy meals so we signed up for a program that provided food. Every Friday morning, they brought a week's worth of frozen meals. Mama loved them and it made things so much easier for us. I chopped the entrées and added a little chicken broth to keep them moist. So all Jackie had to do was heat them up.

Even though Mama was eating, she was losing weight. She was eating enough, but not as much as she used to. Also, we read that as the disease progressed, the digestive system would fail to absorb the nutrients. So even what she did eat wouldn't benefit her as it should.

DOWNHILL

She was changing so fast. It was apparent she was going downhill fast. I wanted to let the grandkids know what was going on. I know how much they love Nanny and Papa, so I posted a Note on Facebook.

How Mama is Doing (You don't have to read it – It's so sad.) Posted September 2010

Mama is declining. She is weaker. We don't walk at the park any more. We do walk down the street (or road at my house) about half a block down and then back. But she leans to the right and some days she leans on me and her right foot drags a little. Papa takes her around the yard at home sometimes. On days when the weather is bad, I hold both her hands and lead her through the house, me walking backwards, like a dance, until we get tired. Exercise is important to keep the circulation going and the digestion.

 She used to drink lots of water. She would get to the bottom of her big blue cup and make the annoying sound a straw makes at the end of a drink. That was our signal to refill. But she never picks up her glass anymore. Now we pick up the cup between tasks and put the straw to her lips so she can drink. Sometimes we will stand in one spot sipping 'til it's empty. Quite an accomplishment to drink a whole glass. We've added prune juice and G2 to the drink offerings to help with digestion and dehydration.

It's been about a month since she last said someone's name... "Susan." And Papa said one day she said "wet" while taking off her sockies. That was different. She used to say "yeah" and "okay", but now she only says "yeah". We rarely get her to laugh, but smiles are an everyday thing. Last week she laughed when I told Papa how quick she pulled up her bloomers and headed out of the bathroom. I was making a little room in the cabinet and packed up the enema equipment in a Wal-Mart bag and stuck it in the closet. Guess she wanted no part of that.

She loves to eat! Especially sweets and sauces. Why not? She is having a little trouble with her partial making a tender spot on her gums and some loose teeth bother her sometimes. We have been cutting up her sandwiches so she doesn't have to bite down. She can eat half a peanut butter and jelly sandwich by herself with her left hand, but we feed her most of the time. She doesn't use her spoon or fork unless I hold her hand and work it for her. Papa sits on the other side of the table now and just fixes one plate for both of them. He has become quite the cook. Even so, her appetite is not as good as it was, and she has lost down to 136 lbs. Which is not too bad at this point, but is upsetting when we think of what is ahead of us. She has also lost a couple of inches in height.

She still walks pretty well, but is shaky and unbalanced sometimes when she gets up, so we don't let her get too far without chasing her down. We help her sit down on the potty, and help her lay down on the bed or on the couch. She seems to have forgotten how to position herself to lie down. For some reason, this is traumatic for me to think about. So we have to lean her over on her pillow and we swing her legs around, otherwise she just falls back on the bed all stiff holding her head up and can't relax. I have a cot in my spare room now for the nights she is with me.

She always smiles when I pretend the little stuffed puppy nips me on the neck, and she smiles when Papa gives her sugar. She still knows so much about what is going on. She is so brave. We think she has headaches sometimes, but no severe pain and we are thankful for that. I think she has aged 10 years in the last year. We will do the best we can. Pray for us all.

THE BEST IS BEHIND US

We weren't sure how much time we had left, but we knew if she kept losing weight that it wouldn't be long. Neither of us wanted to think of what was coming. We knew we were going to lose her, but we didn't know how. Would she get pneumonia or have a heart attack? Would she fall and break a bone? Would she develop an infection? Or would she just waste away?

We reminded ourselves how many people are suffering in this world and realized that many of them have a similar illness. Millions of families are trying to care for loved ones with terminal illnesses. We told ourselves, "We can do this. If we have to go through this, God will give us strength." And we are not alone.

In God's amazing love for us he has given us his Word, the Bible, to encourage us.

For I am persuaded, that neither death, nor life, nor

angels, nor principalities, nor powers, nor things present, nor things to come, nor height, nor depth, nor any other creature, shall be able to separate us from the love of God, which is in Christ Jesus our Lord.

Romans 8:38-39

DID SHE HAVE A STROKE?

When Mama showed signs of weakness on her right side in October, we wondered if she had suffered a stroke. She was definitely leaning to the right when she walked and her mouth was drooping a little. It seemed we were constantly wiping the corner of her mouth. I started throwing a hand towel over her shoulder like she used to do when she was cooking, so it would be handy. The more we looked at her, the more we believed she could have had a stroke, but we weren't sure what to do. We knew that as she got worse that anything could go wrong. She didn't seem to have any pain. We really didn't think there was anything they could do for her even if it was a stroke. But we decided to go anyway. Her doctor said they may want to adjust her medicine and sent her to get a CT scan of her brain.

It was an ordeal. We had already been to the doctor and now we were at the hospital, waiting again for the CT. We were off our eating schedule and Mama was getting anxious. She was pacing. I took her to the hall to work off a little nervous energy. Three people asked if we needed anything while we were out in the hall. We got her a soft drink, but it was in a can and she wasn't used to drinking without a straw and we dribbled down the front of her top. Finally, they took her back. They only let one of us go back with her, so Jackie went with her. Then they had to get help, because she didn't understand she needed to lie still and they needed someone to hold her.

Finally, we headed home. All of us were exhausted and swore we wouldn't put her through any more tests. When the doctor called with results, we talked about our decision not to do further testing and we all agreed it was the best thing for her. The CT scan showed no sign of stroke, but confirmed a general atrophy of the brain.

HEAVY METAL POISONING?

After a few failed attempts, I did learn to take out and put in her partial. As I handled the appliance, I thought about the glob of metal that rested against the roof of her mouth all day. I recalled hearing about the possibility of getting mercury poisoning from fillings disturbed during dental work and wondered what kind of metal was used to make her partial. I did some research and discovered that mercury amalgam is used in fillings and in other dental work. I remembered how proud she was of her new teeth. She had quite a bit of work done over a period of a couple of years to get it completed. And it was soon after that she started having problems.

What if this was heavy metal poisoning? Her symptoms were a little different from Alzheimer's and it started so early. I still wanted it to be something that could be fixed. I ordered a test from a website to check for heavy metals.

Actually, I ordered two, one for her and one for me to see if there would be a difference. And there was. Mine showed low concentrations of metals and hers was high. I took pictures of the test and called her neurologist. We took her in and they had us send a urine sample off to be analyzed. It came back negative for heavy metals.

There was nothing else to try. Even if the test had come back positive I wondered how much of the damage could have been reversed. I gave up my search for a cure.

MORE CHANGES

Since Mama was having trouble swallowing her pills, we had stopped giving her the ibuprofen. We also stopped giving her the water pill that was for her blood pressure. She had lost so much weight that her blood pressure was lower. And she was drinking less water. Dehydration was the issue we were concerned with now instead of high blood pressure. I started giving her Liqua Lea, a liquid vitamin supplement from Shaklee, hoping her body would be able to absorb some of the goodness.

She kept taking out her partial and if it was in, she just let it hang loose in her mouth. It didn't fit right now that she was losing weight and it rubbed her gums until they were sore. We had been chopping her food anyway, so we let her do without it. She was a little self conscious about her missing front teeth, but we were used to seeing our snaggletooth Nanny without her teeth and we didn't even notice.

Her glasses were bothering her. She kept taking them off,

so we let her do without them too.

Smooth, thick foods were easier for her to swallow, so we decided to have mashed potatoes more often. It was one of her favorite foods and we had stopped making them when we found out she had diabetes. Now, she needed those carbohydrates and her Metformin was keeping her blood sugar under control. We added tomato juice and buttermilk to the menu.

She was getting more rigid. We were helping her up and down now. She could still get up from the table and if she tried hard enough, she could get up from the couch by herself, but we had to help her when it was time to lie down. She had forgotten how to get situated. She would sit on the edge of the bed and fall back with her legs still hanging off the side. She would hold her head up until we could help her get turned around. Papa said she, "looked like a little turtle on a log." We tried to be gentle and move her slowly. We got better at it as the days went by.

Towards the end of the summer of 2010 she had stopped taking her sweater off if she got too warm. One afternoon, I noticed the back of her hair was damp with sweat and realized we would have to take over the temperature control. We would be more conscious of it now. We could always tell if she was getting too cool. Her hands would get cold first. We checked them often.

A few years ago, when I was visiting with Aunt Helen and Uncle Butch, they gave me a beanbag hand-warmer. It looked like a little flannel pillow, but was filled with dry beans. You microwave it for one minute and it stays warm for quite a while. It came in handy now. Mama would usually lie down after we had been out for a walk or after a meal. At her house she would rest on the couch, at my house she would lie down in her bed. Then we would cover her hands with the hand warmer and over that we would lay her fusia robe or one of the beautiful afghans she had knitted in better times.

We had been using the potty chair Dad brought us for awhile now. At night Papa kept it by her bed. During the day it sat over the toilet. At first, she used the handles to let herself down and it wasn't as low as the toilet seat so that helped. But now she was forgetting to hold on and she would just fall back against the tank, so we had to stand beside her and help ease her down. At night, she had trouble bending her knees. It was a challenge to get her in position before an accident happened. We just did the best we could.

In the afternoons, she would get disoriented. She would stand looking at a picture or a knick knack on the entertainment center like she'd never seen it before. She would wander through the house, carrying her napkin, looking up at the corners of the ceiling. We asked her if she could see her angels.

She could say so much with her eyes. We learned how to read her expressions. One day when she gave Jackie that lost look that said, "What's happening to me?" Jackie just broke down. He knelt down in front of her by the couch and put his head in her lap and cried. She took both of her little hands and began to pet the back of his neck.

149

COOLER WEATHER

Mama loved being outside. If it was cool, I would put her fleece jacket on her with a scarf over her head and around her neck. She didn't mind the cold if the wind wasn't blowing. Lots of days, we would walk twice a day. When we went for our walks down the block, I would tuck my arm under hers, so I could hold her up if she stumbled. She would hold her hands together tightly to keep them from shaking. I filled our walks with, "I wonder what kind of tree that is," and, "Look, her roses are still blooming," and "I like her fall decorations. Don't you?"

There was a giant sycamore tree in the yard of the house behind Mama and Jackie's. The good neighbors had moved away and the house was for sale. Leaves were piling up knee high in the yard. As we neared, Mama focused her attention on the leaves and veered towards the yard. I giggled as we kicked our way through the crunching leaves.

As the nights got colder, Papa went back to the second hand stores on a mission to find pajamas for Mama. I was amazed at what he came back with. After a couple of trips, we had four nearly new pairs of flannel pajamas. He was careful to get only those that buttoned in the front. Mama was having trouble raising her arms over her head which made it difficult to get clothes on and off. Marty gave her a pair of pajamas she said she didn't need any more. They were so soft and were lime green with smiling brown monkey faces all over! They were Mama's favorite, most comfortable pajamas.

150

There were so many nice days that autumn. I wanted to take Mama back to the park, but was afraid she would fall. I didn't want to take her by myself, so I asked Jackie if he would go with us to the park. We made it all the way down to our bench. We sat under the blue, blue sky and looked out across our little lake and watched the geese fussing on the bank. For a moment it seemed nothing had changed. But I held her arm tightly, so she wouldn't fall as we dodged the duck droppings on the sidewalk on our way back to the car. I knew, but didn't dare dwell on the fact that this was our last walk at the park.

HEALING

Cleaning the kitchen is always more fun with music. I put on Kari Jobe. Her clear, worshipful, melody filled the room. Mama stood at the front window captivated, listening, looking far into the pasture across the road. The second song began to play. It is called "Healer". Mama turned and tried to say something. Her mouth kept moving. There was a longing in her expression. As I watched her try to speak my heart broke for her.

I was having a hard time reconciling my faith and reality. I knew in my heart that God could heal her, but it wasn't happening. I wanted so much for her to be whole again. Back when Mama first started crying so much, Jackie and I had a conversation. He said, "I think she was praying that day on the bed, crying and screaming as loud as she could; trying to get God to hear her." We had all been praying in our own way. Having faith, knowing God could heal her, that the miracle could come any day and watching for the

151

signs of improvement. Sometimes there would be improvement, but it would only last a couple of weeks and then there would be a downturn.

As she stood there in front of the living room window trying to tell me what was in her heart I wondered, *What was she trying to say? Was she asking me why she wasn't receiving the healing we wanted so badly? Or was she saying, 'It doesn't matter now. Jesus, is all I need.'*

I tried to comfort her. She came to me in the kitchen. I took her hands in mine and with tears streaming down my face I told her, "Mama, soon we'll have new bodies. It won't be long now. Until then, we have today. No one knows when their last day will be. We don't know what tomorrow will bring, but we know the Lord with be with us."

> *Behold, I tell you a mystery; We shall not all sleep, but we shall all be changed - In a moment, in the twinkling of an eye, at the last trumpet. For the trumpet will sound, and the dead will be raised incorruptible, and we shall be changed.*
>
> *I Corinthians 15:51-52*

A BAD FALL

It would be Thanksgiving soon and we weren't really in the mood for celebrations. Jackie's birthday had come and gone without much ado. We were trying to keep our chins up, and holidays were especially hard emotionally. It was easier to think of them as just another day. My sister, Jack, was due for a visit, and she had a plan. She wanted to prepare chicken and dressing, with all the fixings and bring it down for Thanksgiving. It sounded great to me. It would be good to see her and Ricky. Mama would love some chicken and dressing.

I think it was John Lennon that said, "Life is what happens to you while you are making other plans."

On the Tuesday before Thanksgiving, I was cutting a couple of inches off the bottom of Mama's pajama pants. We had been turning them up and I decided to hem them. I was in the utility room and laid the pajamas out on the ironing board to do the cutting. As I finished, I said, "Let's show Papa," and carried them toward the living room where Jackie was sitting. Mama was a few steps ahead of me. She stopped just inside the living room by the end table and turned to look at me. I guess she turned too fast. She lost her balance and fell backwards onto the end table, upsetting the lamp and everything on the table. Her legs went up in the air and then she rolled off the side of the table and fell right on her face. Her reflexes were so slow that she didn't even raise her arms to catch herself. We were only two steps away. One of us on either side of her, but neither of us could stop her. Both of us were kneeling at her side immediately, hoping she didn't break her neck.

Her eyes were open, and she tried to raise her head. Thank God she was moving! But we told her, "Don't try to move, Mama. We're gonna get some help."

She was bleeding badly from her nose and mouth and a tooth was lying on the carpet. Her nose was swollen and we believed it could be broken. I held her while Jackie ran to get a towel to put under her face. I reached over for the phone that had fallen off the end table and called 911. We sat with her, holding and petting her, reminding her not to move until the ambulance got there.

The EMTs were very careful and thorough. They worked together to get her onto the stretcher without causing any further distress. They secured her head and neck with a brace and strapped her onto the board. It was good to know she couldn't move until we could find out if anything was broken, but now that she was on her back, I had a feeling of panic, knowing she could easily choke on the blood. I explained about her dementia, that she couldn't speak, and that she was having problems swallowing. They assured me they would examine her mouth carefully for any other loose teeth and that they would be able to suction the blood out when they got her to the ambulance.

I sat in the passenger seat of the ambulance, making phone calls. The sound of the motor and equipment drowned out all the voices around me. Neighbors were coming to see if they could help. Looking to the back of the ambulance, I could see the EMT working on Mama's mouth. I could see her eyes blink. My heart broke as I saw Jackie cup his hands around his eyes to peer in the back window of the ambulance. He was trying to get a glimpse of his "little girl." That's what he called her when she was having a hard time, "She's just Papa's little girl. That's all she is. Just Papa's little girl."

I was reminded of the picture of Mama as a toddler that

sits on Jackie's bedside table. I wondered if she knew what was coming when she framed it and put it there and if she knew how he would care for her.

THE HOSPITAL

Susan met us at the hospital and we spent a few miserable hours with Mama strapped down on that board in a room at the ER. They took her back to x-ray her face and neck and told us when they got the results we could unstrap her. Her mouth was still bleeding. As far as we could tell, most of it was coming from her gums where her tooth was knocked out. There were a few cuts on the inside of her lips too. We had to keep the blood suctioned. Amazingly, Mama didn't get choked.

We were worried she would start getting nervous. She had missed a dose of Risperidal. But she held together. And thank the Lord, nothing was broken.

Finally, they took off the straps and took the board away. I tried to clean up the blood on her face with a damp wash cloth a dab at a time. They wanted to do an x-ray of her chest. That was fine. Her white blood cell count was up. They were looking for infection. As we waited for the results, tension built. We knew there was a risk of pneumonia developing with all the choking and swallowing problems she was having. I thought about all the years of smoking and the possibility of lung cancer was in the back of my mind. It would be good to know. The x-rays of her chest came back clear.

I am so glad Susan was there. She brought calm to the

155

room. Jackie and I were frazzled and traumatized from the ordeal. When they wanted to do more tests, to find out why her white blood cell count was up, I protested. I understand, the doctor was responsible to be sure everything was thoroughly investigated, but we knew that her time was short, and that there were going to be things that would go wrong. Her body was failing. We were at the point where we had to start letting go. Of course, we wanted to keep her as comfortable as possible and wanted to keep pain and suffering to a minimum. Right now, if nothing was broken, that meant getting her home as soon as possible.

Mama kept trying to get off the bed. She wanted out of there. It had been days since she had let loose with a scream. I wondered how much she could take. She was getting very agitated. Susan tried to calm her. She held her hands and sang to her. We had to work at keeping things under control. They already wanted to admit her. I was afraid to think what a battle it would be to get her home if she broke down.

I told them clearly we were ready to go. They responded, "You don't want to admit her?" We felt like they were questioning our judgment. Susan, Jackie and I discussed what was happening. They were taking too long. We understood they are geared to caring for patients that will benefit from extensive diagnostics because they are going to get better. We were only trying to keep her as comfortable as possible while she died. We knew it was just a matter of time. She was already starting to waste away. Prolonging the inevitable now would only increase the suffering.

We were also aware that the staff would always be on the alert for any signs of abuse. People who care for the elderly are stretched thin at times and some become abusive. We knew they had to consider it with the type of injuries Mama had and the fact that she couldn't talk made it harder for them to trust us. I appreciated their concern, but it was only causing more stress. If they only knew how badly we wanted to get her home where she would feel safe and relax so we could take care of her better.

After the shift change, we pressed them for a reason to delay any longer. A new doctor wanted us to tell him exactly what happened. We recounted again how she fell. As we explained our situation, Susan, apparently the only sane person in the room took up for us. She offered that Mama was, "one of the lucky ones, that didn't have to go to a nursing home."

RECOVERING

We were glad to be home. I put antibiotic ointment on Mama's skinned up nose and cheek with Q-tips. We gave her drops of water from a straw and enough yogurt to get her pills down and went to bed. I would stay with her the next two nights. It was so hard on her, we didn't know if she would make it. She had no appetite. No wonder after swallowing all the blood. She was weak. Her blood pressure was running lower and all she wanted to do was rest. Bless her heart; we weren't sure if she knew what had happened. She seemed more disoriented than ever.

Her nose was so swollen she was breathing through her

mouth. At night, her tongue would get coated with a whitish film. I tried to moisten and clean her tongue with a Q-tip. After a couple of nights of that, I realized she wasn't clearing her mouth of the yogurt and it had her crushed pills in it. It was drying on her tongue. We started giving her pills a little earlier to give her more time to clear her mouth before lying down at night. As her mouth healed, I got some tiny soft toothbrushes to clean her mouth with.

We worried about pain, and gave her children's ibuprofen. She would raise her hand to her head and touch the side of her face. We decided that meant she was hurting.

And we were blaming ourselves, but neither of us blamed the other. We had to weigh our options. We could no longer let her have the freedom to walk around. Would we need to restrain her, or take her to a nursing home? We resolved, if she came out of this strong enough to walk, we would never let her take a step alone. We would restrain her if that's what it took. We knew they would restrain her in a nursing home. Better for it to be at home.

On Wednesday, I fed her some mashed potatoes for lunch and helped her lie down on the couch. While I cleaned up the kitchen, every few minutes I would peek in the living room to see how she was doing. The phone rang. It was Jack, calling from Muskogee to see how Mama was doing. As we talked, I heard a little cough, so I stepped into the living room and saw that Mama was throwing up. I threw the phone down on the couch as I dove toward Mama. She was just lying there with vomit foaming down her chin and neck and running onto the pillow. She was struggling to breathe. It was horrible to think she couldn't respond to what was happening. I rolled her over so that her head was over the edge of the couch and with a Kleenex from the end table I started trying to clear her mouth. She was fine. It was messy, but she was fine. *What's next?* I thought.

I called Jack back to let her know Mama was okay and we would look forward to seeing her and Ricky in the morning, on Thanksgiving.

That night, as I stood over her in the dark with the antibiotic ointment, I quietly told her, "I'm gonna put some more medicine on your face."

My long hair was hanging loose in the space above her as I leaned over her. She reached up and passed her hand through my hair, letting it flow between her fingers, slowly slipping strand by strand back into place. Emotion froze my throat and tears burned my eyes. *I wonder if this is the last time she will be able to show that she loves me. How much more time do we have?*

THANKSGIVING

Mama was improving a little every day. We were telling her what a good dinner Jack and Ricky were bringing her.

It took both of them three trips to bring all the dishes in the house. We asked if they needed any help, but they just kept saying, "No, we've got it."

Then Jack sat down to hold Mama. It had been a while

since they had seen her. If only they could have seen her before she fell. Her hair was at just the right length and had just enough body to make it look nice. Everyone told her what beautiful hair she had. And the weight she lost, even though it worried us, made her look more like she did when she was younger, when she and Jackie married. Now her lip was swollen, her nose and cheek were scabbing, her jaw and chin were bruised, and she was weak from all she had been through.

It took Mama a minute or two to remember. Jack realized from the first look Mama gave her that she couldn't place them. But as Jack asked her how she was doing, the familiar voices and laughter pulled up pleasant memories and she smiled. Ricky and I got dinner warmed up while Jack held Mama and visited with her dad. When it was ready to eat, we told Jack, "We have rules around here, and one of them is no crying at the table, so dry it up. It's time to eat."

Dinner was as delicious as we were hungry. I fixed Mama a plate, chopping as finely as I could. We tried using a blender, but it didn't work well for such small portions, so I kept chopping. Jack insisted on feeding Mama. It was nice to have a break. Mama's appetite was still not up to par, so she only ate a little, but she enjoyed it and we had plenty of leftovers for later.

After dinner, the guys were visiting in the living room while Mama rested on the couch. So Jack and I slipped into the back bedroom to talk. We laughed as we caught each other up on our adventures through life. Then we talked about Mama. I showed her the section on Letting

Go in *Coach Broyles' Playbook for Alzheimer's Caregivers*. She told me about her Aunt Bonnie, a family friend who stayed with Jack when she could no longer take care of herself. It was Aunt Bonnie's wish to die at home, or Jack's home, and to not be put on life support. Jack talked about hospice and how much they helped her at the end. We agreed it was time to start looking at hospice and what they could offer. We needed to start planning for the end. I asked her how long she thought we had left with Mama, "Do you think we will still have her in the spring?"

Jack replied, "I'm no doctor, and I haven't got much to base my guess on, but judging by how much weight she is losing and how little she is taking in, I don't see how she could last much more than a couple of months."

I agreed. "That's what I was thinking. Her birthday is at the end of January."

It was amazing how she bounced back. Jack stayed with her Thanksgiving night. Then through the weekend, I stayed with her. Until she gained some strength and was eating better we didn't want to take any chances. Her swallowing was worse than before the fall and she was choking easily. When she got strangled, we would lean her over on her side so the liquid would run back out. We weren't sure if it would get better or not, but after a few days she had improved to the point where we decided I could stay home at night and we would get back on our regular schedule. I was exhausted.

KEEPING HER SAFE

As Mama got stronger, she would rock forward when she wanted to get up. I would help her up and walk her around the house until she was tired. We watched her as she gained strength, wondering if she would be able to get up by herself soon. We reminded her not to get up without us. We didn't want her to fall. In the kitchen, she would lean to the right in her chair. In her sewing room, we found a long piece of cloth that would serve as a sash. We wrapped the bulky material around the back of the chair and around her waist and tied it in a big knot in her lap. She could untie it if she wanted to. Mostly, it was there to remind her to stay seated. Still it wasn't enough. We were afraid she would fall sideways and tip the chair over, so when she was at the table, we would put the sash around her and pull a chair up on either side of her chair. Now she was safe and would stay put while we fixed something to eat.

She would put her shaking hands on the edge of the table and they would tap tap tap tap tap. Papa said she was playing her piano.

We were worried that she would fall out of bed at night. She would put one leg off the edge and start working her way over. We didn't want to take any chances. We priced new bed rails. The kind that has an arm that folds out and slides under the mattress, like you would use to keep the kids from falling out of bed. At the pharmacy, Jackie was explaining to them what we were looking for and one of the ladies working there said she had one at home in the shed that no one was using and he was welcome to it. *Praise the Lord!* So we had a bed rail. It was just enough to discourage her from trying to get up.

We let her try to use a walker. She was willing, but she was a terrible driver. She couldn't maneuver around the furniture. So we ordered a wheelchair. Jackie cried. He said it was like giving up. Mama gave me a look that told me she didn't like the idea either, but I told them we wouldn't have to use it all the time - that it would give us options. It would be a safe place for her to sit and we could move her around and keep her with us as we worked around the house. And it would be good to have if we went anywhere.

I ended up using it more than Jackie did. I would park her in the utility room while I folded clothes and at my house, I would move her from the table to the sunshine at the back door. At her home she would sit on the couch a lot. And Jackie would sit with her. They would sit there looking out the front window, him holding her hands to keep them still, telling her how much he loved her and what a good girl she was. When it was time to go to bed, she would be so tired, she would forget to move her feet. Papa would help her stand up, then hold her and walk backwards, dragging her along to bed. I showed him how to put her in the chair, so he could roll her in there, but he wouldn't do it.

During that time I started getting a feeling of dread in the morning when it was time to go over there. I was ashamed of the way I felt, but it was getting harder and harder to face. When I was away, I wanted to run from it, but when I was there, I didn't want to leave. "This is hard to do, hard to see," I told Papa, "but if she has to go

163

through this, we will go through it with her. We will be strong, as strong as we have to be."

He agreed.

STILL GOING

Packing was getting to be an ordeal. Besides the usual things, we had added more clothes for cooler weather. I also took her hand warmer, prune juice, her frozen meals, the potty chair, her wheelchair, and a shower chair. It was harder to get her in the Jeep now too. I would help her get her left leg in and let her rest on my knee while I tried to scoot her in. I would get her as far as I could and then Jackie would work on it a little. Finally, we would get her far enough in to close the door. A little patience goes a long way. Most of the time if you waited a minute, she would move to make herself more comfortable. She helped us less and less as time went on. I discovered I could put a towel across the seat and when I got her on the edge of the seat, if I had someone to support her; I could go around to the driver's side and pull the towel towards me, bringing her with it. Each week I wondered if we would be able to do it again.

Jackie decided to trade his truck for something Mama could get into a little easier. Usually, it was my Jeep we were travelling in. And if I was honest with myself, I didn't really think she would be with us past spring, but I didn't have the heart to say it. If he wanted to trade his truck for a car, let him do it. I didn't say a word.

We would still enjoy the sunshine whenever we could.

One day at my house, we walked down to the end of the porch to sit in the sunshine. She got to the end and stood there in the sunlight with her eyes closed holding onto the rail. She liked for me to sing to her. I sang the beautiful old hymns we loved so much: "Great is Thy Faithfulness" and "Fairest Lord Jesus". I wondered how much longer we would have her. I thought of our family. Some may have seen her for the last time already.

As we rode in the car on the way home, we listened to Christian radio. Chris Tomlin was singing "I Will Rise". When he started the chorus Mama raised up as straight as she could in her seat. I chuckled the first time, thinking it was a coincidence, but after four or five times I started crying. "Yes, Mama. We're going to rise. You are ready to go, aren't you?" She was looking forward to a better place.

HOW DO YOU DIE?

You can find out about anything on the Internet. I started researching what hospice could do for us. I had heard that the doctor would have to say she had six months or less to live before it would be approved. But Mama and Jackie's neighbor, Arvilla, had been on hospice longer than that. She had leukemia.

Hospice could offer whatever level of help we would need including advice and medical care. We didn't know what we would need, because we didn't know what was going to happen. I talked to Jackie and Susan and we decided we were doing okay for now, but realized that if Mama needed any further medical attention we weren't going to be able to take her to the clinic and didn't want another trip to the hospital.

It was hard to talk about it, but we did. There are many ways to die: heart attack, stroke, kidney failure, pneumonia, infection, choking. Some people go faster than others, some have more pain, and some struggle. *Lord, help us to know what to do.*

WINDING DOWN

We did most of our walking in the house those days. I would turn the TV to the Local Government Access channel that shows the community announcements and plays all the oldies. I would sing along and we would walk. I would walk backwards, leading her, holding her hands or forearms in my hands. It was a dance.

We would walk from her room on one end of the house through the living room and utility room to the back bedroom and back again. As we passed through the utility room, her eyes would be glued to her favorite sweater hanging on the hook on back of the sewing room door. When she fell at Thanksgiving, the EMT had made a crooked cut from the bottom of her sleeve to the top. We washed it and hung it there, unwilling to attempt to mend it, unwilling to throw it away.

In the back bedroom, she would stand beside the big bed that used to be in her room and gently run her hand across the bedspread smoothing the covers. I would ask her if she wanted to rest for awhile. "We can lay down up there." And she would raise her knee. I'd say, "Wait a minute now. Come all the way up here by the pillow and turn around." And I would lead her and help her sit back. Then while she laid back, I would lift her legs and swing her around. Then I would roll her over on her side so she wouldn't be so close to the edge. And she would be there about ten minutes and then she would be ready to go again. Jackie didn't walk with her back and forth through the house like I did, (he said all that dancing made his hips hurt) but he would walk her to the back room and help her get up on the big bed for a few minutes.

When I left them in the afternoon, Mama and Jackie would be sitting on the couch together and when I showed up in the mornings, they would be sitting on the couch in the same place. I'd say, "That's where you were when I left you yesterday!"

For now we kept doing what we were doing. Susan and Bill kept coming to visit even though it broke her heart over and over. I know. It broke mine too. Susan would pay the bills and then she would sit with Mama on the couch and listen to Jackie's stories about then and now. When it was time for them to leave, Mama would reach up to take Bill's hand for a moment.

Jack would call from Muskogee and I would hold the phone up to Mama's ear so she could tell her, "I love you more." Now and then, Marty would bring the boys for a little while and they would look at Nanny with wide eyed questions and concern.

Jackie's sister, also named Glenda, came for a visit. Mama welcomed her with a smile, but looked at her with a wrinkled brow. Glenda said, "You don't remember me do you?" Mama continued to frown. "It's okay, don't worry about it." Glenda tried to comfort her. Things were winding down and it would be Christmas soon.

OLD PICTURES

We sat on the couch together paging through her oldest album of pictures. There were pictures of my mother as a girl, school pictures from the 1950s, and pictures of some of her friends. As I admired her hair, and her clothes, and those smiling green eyes at each stage of her life, I realized one of the pictures I thought was her was not her. One of Mama's friends from school looked so much like her that everyone got them mixed up. Nelda was her name. I said it out loud. Mama gave a blink that was almost a nod. I imagined how it must have been as a teenager back then. No cell phones, no Internet, no phone at all. Barely any TV. No way to get to town.

I picked up a picture of Mama and her friend, Carrie, in their bathing suits, standing up to their knees in a creek with a bluff on the other side of the water. I thought how they must have planned their swimming trip and imagined out loud, "We'll have to go on Saturday afternoon. I have to help Mama put up some green beans first. It's going to be so hot in that kitchen. I can't wait to get to the creek. Oh, and be sure to bring your camera."

I looked at Mama and she nodded.

I continued, "Then when they were at the creek, they probably decided to take a couple of pictures before they

168

got their hair wet."

Mama blinked her eyes in agreement.

HER TOOTH

One day Marty's boys followed me into Mama's room where I was dusting her dresser. Bryson reached for Nanny's glasses and said, "What's sat?"

"That's Nanny's glasses. She doesn't like to wear them anymore."

Layne pointed at the pink cylinder on her jewelry tray, "What's sat?" he asked.

"That's bubbles from Anthony and Cassie's wedding. Do you want to see some bubbles?"

I pulled the tiny wand out and blew bubbles all over the room. They all squealed and giggled, jumping up and scrambling to catch the bubbles. We did that a few times until we attracted Papa's attention. "What's goin' on in here?" he said in his big boss voice.

"They're just curious about Nanny's things," I said.

"What's sat?" Bryson asked again as he pointed to the wax paper envelope on Mama's dresser.

"It's Nanny's tooth." That got their attention. "She knocked her tooth out when she fell and hurt her nose."

Jackie shooed the boys out and told me I could throw the

tooth away if I wanted to. I quickly stuffed it in the middle top drawer with her embroidered handkerchiefs, mumbling something about DNA testing.

A couple of months earlier, I had read about the genetic research that has been done on Alzheimer's disease. The book explained that if your DNA contains a certain genome, the E4, you had a much greater chance of developing the disease. It also brought out the fact that when the disease affects someone at an early age it is more likely to be the result of genetics and more likely to run in the family. We were all aware that Mama was having problems by the time she was 62, which is early.

Would I want to know if I had the gene? If you have the E4 gene, you still might not develop the disease. Would my kids want to know? Maybe they would rather adopt than continue the curse. But Mama has had such a full life. We all must die somehow. If I knew today that I had this disease, would I change anything? No. Well, I would hurry and write this book, before I forget. But none of us have a promise of tomorrow. We should live our lives in such a way that if we are gone next week we can say we did our best. I am reminded of a saying my pastor, Reverend Joe Bisby, posted on the church sign. "Do what you can, with what you have, for those around you." I think that's good advice.

Now that Mama's ashes are in the ground, I guess all we have is a lock of her hair and that silly tooth.

ONE MORE CHRISTMAS

We weren't really in the mood for a holiday, but it was Christmas anyway. There would be no big family gathering this year. Susan and Bill were having their kids and grandchildren over. Jack and Ricky were going to her mom's for Christmas. Marty was traveling to her brother's house for the holiday. Thomas was in Pennsylvania with his sister and his mom. I planned for Austin and his girlfriend Jennifer, Aja and Mike, and Mama and Jackie to eat with us on Christmas day.

I knew this would be the last Christmas I would have with my mother and I wanted it to be special. I decided to make a ham and green beans with mashed potatoes and rolls like she did for so many years. And I made our favorite cheesecake.

The Christmas lights on the front porch brightened our evenings. Every Friday, as soon as it would get dark I would say, "Mama, Glenn's going to turn on the Christmas lights. Look out the window." She would get out of bed to see the lights. If it wasn't too cold we would go out on the porch and walk to the end and back, amazed, surrounded by the magical blinking of the colorful lights. She was enjoying the decorations, even if no one else was.

I worried about Jackie being alone on Christmas Eve. We had decided Mama would stay with me like she usually did on Friday night and Jackie would come over early on Christmas morning to help take care of her so I would be free to cook.

On Christmas Eve, Mama watched me work in the kitchen

from her wheelchair. Then as it grew dark, and all the preparations were finished, we sat in the living room watching the Christmas shows on TV. They were dancing and singing, playing all the old favorites: Bing Crosby singing "White Christmas" and Nat King Cole singing, "The Christmas Song." Now that I wasn't busy cooking, I could realize how much I would miss her and my throat tightened as I tried to hold back the tears.

After a little while, Mama wanted to get up. She had been in her chair for a while. It was time to stretch her legs, so I helped her up and began to walk her around the room. Glenn had already gone to bed, or at least to the bedroom. As we waltzed around and around the couch to those old familiar songs in the dim light of the TV and the Christmas tree, I quietly cried. She still loved life so much. Even as limited as it was. There was still so much to enjoy and be thankful for.

She cried too. She didn't make tears anymore, but she cried. And it wasn't a good thing. I guess the extra fluid in her throat caused her to start coughing and she couldn't stop. I took her to her room and tried to help her calm down. I tried to lay her down on her side thinking it might clear better, but it made it worse. I got a cold washcloth and wiped her face and mouth and held it on her neck. I took off her sweater and her slippers and socks because she was getting too hot and was starting to sweat.

When she coughed, it sounded like gurgling in her throat and she couldn't get it cleared. It was alarming. And then she started expelling stringy white froth. Over and over, I reached in her mouth with a Kleenex to clear as much as I could. There were a couple of times she could hardly catch her breath. I was afraid she might die right then on Christmas Eve. I prayed, *God, help me to know what to do!* I thought about calling an ambulance, but I knew what it would be like at the hospital. I knew if I could just get her to stop coughing for a while, the fluids would settle back down. So I told her, "Just try to hold it for a minute while I fix some honey and lemon." I gave her two or three drops at a time. I don't know if it was the honey and lemon or the prayer or just the effort to suppress the coughing, but she started getting better. I'm sure it was the combination of all of them.

We sat on the edge of the bed for an hour while she held back the cough. She was afraid to lie down, but she was so exhausted she couldn't sit up. She kept falling back. So I put a stack of pillows behind her and put my arm around her and held her there until finally she relaxed enough to lie down and go to sleep.

Christmas was nice. The kids were a little quieter than usual. I know it was hard for them to see Nanny like she was. Aja wore a halo of stars and Mike brought antlers and took pictures of our lab Lucy wearing them. Austin and Jennifer were dropping hints about getting engaged. At the table, Papa and I sat on either side of Nanny. We took turns helping her eat. After dinner, we opened our presents. Then we had cheesecake for dessert. Mama licked her lips. Everybody loved the cheesecake. Happy Birthday Jesus!

NOT SO HAPPY NEW YEAR

I was on my way home from dropping off Mama on New Year's Day and I called Glenn to see if he needed me to stop and get anything at the store. He sounded a little flat, so I asked him how he was doing. He said, "Not too good." Now that wasn't normal.

"What's wrong?" I asked.

"My chest is hurting. I don't feel so good."

He talked me out of calling 911 and I hurried to get home. He said he had taken an aspirin and an antacid and was waiting for it to work. When I got there he was lying on the couch. He was pale and his skin was damp. I knew something was wrong, but he didn't want me to call for help. All he could think about was that we needed to be in Little Rock at the airport in just a few hours to pick up Thomas who was flying home from Pennsylvania.

We live out in the country and it's about twenty-five miles to the hospital. I told Glenn that I would go get Thomas myself if I had to, but he needed to see a doctor and we headed for town. As we drove we made arrangements for someone to pick Thomas up and then we rushed the rest of the way to the hospital. Glenn had 100% blockage in his right coronary artery and he was having a heart attack. As they took him back to try to clear the blockage, one of the nurses pointed out the way to the waiting room, "Down the long hall and out the doors to the left."

As soon as they wheeled the bed out of my sight, I began

to sob. I prayed, *Lord, surely you won't take him now. I love him so much.* I couldn't stand the thought of losing him.

After I stopped crying enough to talk, I made a few calls. It wasn't long before Aja and Mike were there. Soon Glenn's sisters arrived and I was surrounded by concerned family. The doctor was able to open the blockage and insert a stent without major surgery. They released him to go home two days later. Thankfully, he would recover well over the next few months.

SUPPORT

Over the next couple of weeks, I spent less time with Mama and more time helping Glenn get adjusted to new medications and making sure he didn't overdo it. Susan spent extra time with Mama and ran errands for Jackie. Marty checked in more often and Jack came down from Muskogee to help for a few days. That first week, Mama did without her shower; they made do with what we call a spit bath. Jackie would run a sink full of warm water and wash her face and hands, under her arms and her bottom. He was a pro at getting her cleaned up.

The second week, I would go by Mama's long enough to get her ready for her day, then I would head home to make sure Glenn was okay. We needed some backup. We were all stretched about as far as we could stretch. We decided to see if we could get started with hospice. It wouldn't hurt for Mama to get familiar with someone else who could provide personal care or anything else in case something happened to Jackie or me. What if one of us got sick? Or was in an accident? We needed someone else to know the routine. And the coughing was getting worse. She hadn't had a bad spell like on Christmas Eve, but you could hear the congestion when she would get strangled. We thought surely they would know what to do. We had no experience with this.

I called the Alzheimer's hotline. I wondered what other people did when swallowing and choking became a problem. I explained that as the swallowing problems had worsened she had been losing weight. I told them that we were thickening her liquids and giving her small amounts of food at a time. They were very understanding and supportive, but sadly, they could offer no solutions. They explained that as the disease progressed, the muscles in her throat would stop working. She would lose the ability to control them and the natural reflex that keeps saliva out of her air passages would fail.

I started calling hospice providers. We needed to make a decision. As I discussed our situation with each one, I narrowed down the choices.

EATING AND DRINKING LESS

Over the last few months, she had lost twenty pounds. She was eating less and less. We would feed her until she showed signs of coughing and then we would stop. We offered food every two hours or so, but she wasn't eating very much. We kept a towel handy to wipe up the food that would fly everywhere when she would cough. It was startling at first, to get an eye full of sweet potatoes, or yogurt, but we got used to it. Papa would say, "Nanny, just go ahead and cough it all over Pam. We don't care."

"Thanks, Papa. At least you are wearing glasses," I replied.

Since Christmas, we had been using a Rival food processor that was small enough to puree a half a cup at a time. It was perfect. It was a gift to Susan from her daughter-in-law, Brandi. Susan said we needed it worse than she did and that she would get another. Evidently, it is hard to find anything that will process such a small amount. We went from knife and cutting board to slap-chop and then the little food processor.

Mama was eating and drinking so little we wondered how long she could live on such a small amount Papa was worrying about her not getting enough and he was afraid she would feel hungry. I read to him out of *Coach Broyles' Playbook for Alzheimer's Caregivers*. Literature from the Alzheimer's Association said the same - that when she is eating less she will need less and want less. At this point food is becoming a problem. *She didn't act like she was starving.*

We felt bad about eating in front of her. We would wait until she was resting to eat our lunch. Sometimes we were so busy we didn't eat like we should have. Both Jackie and I were losing weight. In the evening, he was waiting until after he put her to bed to eat. I remember feeling guilty when I would show up in the morning with my purse and my water bottle. She would look at my bottle as I passed and I would hide it beside the refrigerator where she couldn't see it.   We tried to give her liquids. Jackie started off every day with a cup of G2 Gatorade. I added water or chicken broth to all her foods when I pureed it. We dropped thickened juice or water from a straw into her mouth like a mama bird feeding her babies. But sadly, it wasn't enough.

We accepted it. We knew this was part of it, but it was hard. We just kept doing the best we could, giving her as much as we could, and let it take its course.

We kept trying to give her a half a cup of prune juice every day, but we were doing good to get a fourth a cup down her. I usually gave her the liquid vitamins before the prune juice to help wash the taste out. One morning as I poured a spoonful, I accidently knocked the open bottle of vitamins into the dishwater. I quickly grabbed it out of the water, but it was too late. Mama followed me with her eyes as I threw the bottle away. "Well, I guess we don't need that anymore."

She wasn't using as many pads since she was drinking less. And Jackie didn't have to worry about accidents at night now. It made things easier in a way, but knowing the reason why, we weren't happy about it.

I talked to the doctor's office about her pills. They wanted us to keep giving her the heart regulator. And we were still giving her the Risperidal, Metformin for diabetes, and Benadryl to sleep. We could crush everything but the heart regulator. Somehow, we managed to get it down her.

Jack came to visit after being away for a couple of weeks and before we had a chance to warn her, she gave Mama a drink out of the straw. Mama got too much in her mouth and gulped it down. Whew. That was close.

One afternoon, I sat at the kitchen table with Mama. I had just finished wiping buttermilk off the table and my face and said, "Okay, now what are we going to do?"

She just looked at me, probably wondering what I would do next.

I was feeling pretty beat up, so I said, "Why don't we pray? We could use a little prayer couldn't we?"

She blinked.

I took a deep breath and tried to gather my thoughts. I reached deep into my heart and closed my eyes and leaned my head down over the table. What came out, surprised us both. It was a long low wail, "Oooooohhhhhh." I looked up with sad eyes and said, "That's all I have."

She started laughing. She was looking at me as if she knew just how I felt.

PUPPIES

The neighbors' little Shiatsu finally had her puppies. We started seeing the mama with them out in the sunshine after New Years. It was a little warmer out and Mama and I ventured out of the yard and walked down the street a little ways. We didn't walk very far before we decided to go back. We turned around and then we saw the family was outside with the puppies. As we neared the corner, Mama wasn't taking her eyes off the little fluff balls. "We've been waiting to see your puppies. Can we hold one?" They were going to give them away. But we knew

Papa wouldn't take one. It had been about a year since Forrest had died, and he said he wasn't going to have another dog. It hurt too much. They let us hold one of the puppies while we visited over the chain link fence. I held it up to Mama's cheek and it started licking her with its soft little tongue. She looked over at me with a twinkle in her eye and gave a little smile.

BUTTERFLIES AND FLOWERS

A couple of weeks after Glenn's heart attack I decided to take a break and go shopping. For Christmas, he had given me a gift card from Bath & Body Works and I was anxious to spend it. Aja and Mike met me for lunch at the mall. When I shop for lotion, I have to sample every new scent in the store until finally my nose is so confused I can't make a decision. So I end up getting the same fragrance I have at home. This time, though, one of the first scents I tried was called Butterfly Flowers. It was lovely. It made me think of geranium, lilacs, and roses all at the same time. I knew Mama would love it. So I got it for her. Glenn was very generous when he purchased my gift card. I bought something for Aja, Glenn, and myself. It was nice to get out for a change.

Mama was happy to have new lotion. Part of our morning routine was for me to put lotion on her feet and legs before putting on her socks and new pink slippers that Papa had given her for Christmas. As I rubbed the lotion in, I made up a little song.

With butterflies and sunshine
And flowers on her feet
She'll make a good impression
On everyone she meets
And even in the morning
Her smile will be so sweet
With butterflies and sunshine
And flowers on her feet

It was just a cheery little tune. When I got to the word "sweet" I would hold it out and go up at the end. It made her smile, so I sang it every time.

PREDDY DIRLS

When I first started drying Mama's hair, we stood in front of the mirror in the bathroom. As the weeks passed she would get too tired to stand while I fixed her hair, so I would sit her in the desk chair in the living room and take the blow dryer in there. Then as she got weaker and started leaning to the side, we would sit her in her chair at the kitchen table so I could put the sash around her.

Marty and the boys were there one morning as I was finishing up Mama's hair. As I put lotion on her face and hands, Marty told how the boys were saying their Aunt Kim is a "preddy dirl." As we laughed about it one of them piped up and said, "Nanny's a preddy dirl."

"Yes, she is," we all agreed.

Before they left, Marty and the boys followed me to the back bedroom. I helped Mama up on her big bed, and then one at a time I held the boys up to give Mama sweet good-bye kisses.

FALLING INTO MY ARMS

As we walked around the house, we would stop and stand in front of the window in the utility room or the big bed in the back room or the mirror behind the couch in the living room. As I stood behind her one day, she started falling back. Whoa! I caught her and she smiled real big. "You think that's funny? Okay. Try it again. But don't do it until I'm ready." So we started playing a little game. Wherever we stopped, I would stand behind her and she would fall back against me into my arms. I didn't let her fall back very far. Then I would push her back up and she would do it again. Over and over until I said, "That's enough." And I would take her arm or her hands and lead her along.

At some point, to get our minds on pleasant things, I started naming all the flowers I could think of as we stood in front of the window in the living room. When she fell back I said, "Roses." Next time I said, "Lilies." Then I continued with petunias, poppies, irises, daisies, tulips, and carnations. This was our favorite game now: blackberry cobbler, strawberry shortcake, hot fudge sundae, cheesecake.

One evening when Jack was there, during a lull in the conversation I had an idea. Let's play the list game. But instead of me naming things while Mama falls back, let's just go around the room and name celebrities. So Jack started. Funny how your mind goes blank when you are tired and put on the spot.

"Tony Stewart," she said.

Jackie followed with, "Dale Earnhardt."

I came up with, "Elvis Presley." And we went around a couple of times naming presidents and important people. Mama watched us with amusement.

Then Jackie said loudly, "Glenda Swaim!" Mama lit up with a big grin when she heard her name. And we all had a good laugh. It was the perfect ending to our simple game.

GETTING READY

I still took her to spend the night at my house on Friday's. One Saturday we watched Where the Red Fern Grows and one of the songs on the soundtrack is "Sweet Beulah Land", sung by Alison Kraus. When she started singing, Mama started getting excited. She was leaning forward and trying to say something. Her mouth was moving and she had a look of longing on her face. It was Alison Kraus' enchanting voice singing a familiar, hopeful song,

> I'm kind of homesick for a country
> To which I've never been before
> No sad good-byes will there be spoken
> For time won't matter any more

Beulah Land, I'm longing for you
And someday on thee I'll stand
There my home shall be eternal
Beulah Land, sweet Beulah Land

We went to the bedroom and I helped her lay down on the bed. I found the song on the Internet on YouTube. There was another verse.

I'm looking now across that river
Where my faith will end in sight
I've just a few more days to labor
Then I will take my heavenly flight

Beulah Land, I'm longing for you
And someday on thee I'll stand
There my home shall be eternal
Beulah Land, sweet Beulah land

It seemed to me to be the most beautiful song I'd ever heard. I knelt on the floor beside the bed. "I know you are ready to go Mama." She had her hands folded on her tummy. She took a deep breath, and let it out as slow as she could. Then another deep breath and let it out slow again. "I guess you would go right now if you could, wouldn't you?"

She gave a long blink as if to say, "Yes, that's what I'm longing for." And I laid my head on her arm.

We knew the time was getting close when we would have to let her go. Papa would tell me about their talks. He would sit by her in the evenings and tell her how much he loved her and talk about what good times they had. He would tell her he wished he could fix it. But he can't. He would say, "Papa knows he can't keep her."

He didn't stay gone very long on his trips to the store and the pharmacy. He wanted to be there for her if she needed him. It was getting harder for me to leave her everyday. I told her, "You know I want to be there with you, but I can't be here all the time. So if Jesus comes for you, Mama, you go. That will be your time. If Papa can be with you, that will be good. I will be with you if I can. But even if it happens in the middle of the night, it will be alright. You won't be alone. Jesus will be with you."

Jack and Ricky's son, Shawn and his wife Dee Dee came to say good-bye. Shawn was their first grandchild. Mama was lying on the couch in the dim light of the winter evening. Shawn sat in the floor beside her, Dee Dee at her feet. They listened as Papa told about their days, how they sit on the couch together in the evenings and he told them, "This is her life now. This is Nanny's life."

HER BIRTHDAY

Mama's 68th birthday was coming up on Friday. Jackie wanted to order a little cake. We decided I would go ahead and take her home with me on Friday and we would have cake on Saturday when I brought her back. On Friday morning, I stopped at the grocery store and bought her a bright turquoise colored bracelet. I slipped it on her with a kiss and a "Happy Birthday" and told her how pretty she looked. She wasn't smiling as much these days.

185

I did get a laugh out of her in the bathroom at my house that night though. There was a mosquito flitting around on the mirror, so I grabbed the hand towel and started swatting. As I swung the towel, I was saying, "Get outta here you ole black diddo!" When she started laughing, I started laughing. It was such a relief. For that moment, while we were laughing, everything heavy was banished from my mind.

As soon as she got in bed, she started coughing. She sounded awful. You could tell the congestion was worse and as she coughed she was stirring it up and it blocked her air passages so she couldn't get her breath. We had noticed a couple of times in the last week that there would be a tinge of blue around the corners of her mouth. I was seeing it now. It scared her when she couldn't catch her breath. She struggled through an hour of coughing before she went to sleep.

As I knelt beside the bed, I envisioned myself entering the throne room in heaven, carrying her in my arms. As I brought her before the Lord, I knelt respectfully and laid her there. I prayed, *Thank you, Lord for this life. I thank you for the time you have given us with her. But now she is at the end of her life, and she is struggling. Lord, please, look at her life. Examine her and see if there is any reason she must stay here any longer. Surely, it is time for her to go. I trust you, Lord.*

HOSPICE

Saturday morning, she started coughing again. After twenty minutes or so, we found a position that helped her stop. I hurried to get dressed, loaded everything up and took her home. I wasn't about to go through another coughing spell without Papa.

Sunday, Susan brought a beautiful bouquet of flowers. Jack and Susan were both there when she started coughing again. So far Glenn and I had been the only ones to witness her coughing spells. It was very upsetting to see. I told them all about it, but you had to be there to realize how bad it really was. We couldn't deal with this on our own.

We called the hospice company we had chosen and by Wednesday, we had completed the approval process and had all the paperwork done. Jackie bravely signed all the papers specifying do not resuscitate and acknowledging that no life support would be used. They would have someone come by every day to help with personal care. There were nurses available 24/7, there was a social worker to give us emotional support, and a chaplain. They also had beds available at a local hospital where she could stay temporarily if one of us got sick or if she needed medical care that we couldn't provide at home.

The hospice service was in place just in time. As I cleaned her mouth, that morning, I had discovered an infection in one of Mama's teeth. They brought us a liquid antibiotic the next morning. We explained how we were feeding her and giving her liquids by drops from straws and asked if there was anything we could do to help her with swallowing. They told us it might be easier to control how much she was getting if we gave the thickened liquids from a spoon rather than a straw. And they brought oxygen and a suction machine to help clear her throat. They also gave us some liquid hydrocodone to give her if she started coughing again. It was supposed to help her cope with air deprivation and any pain that might occur.

NO MORE PEACHES

For the next two days, we kept the oxygen on her as much as we could. She only coughed a little here and there, but no struggling to breathe like on the weekend. On Friday, our aide, Veronica, came in and helped me give Mama a shower. For the last week or so, she had been so wobbly that Jackie would help me get her over the side of the tub and seated on her shower chair. Then when we were done, I would call him and he would come help get her out. It was the first time anyone but me or Jackie had helped Mama with her shower. It was easier with two. One could hold her and make sure she wasn't going to fall while the other dried and dressed her. After Veronica had gone, Jackie decided to take a trip to Wal-Mart.

It was turning out to be a nice day outside. I wanted to take Mama out on the porch, but was afraid she would fall. So I put her in her wheelchair and rolled her out. She turned her face toward the sun and closed her eyes, soaking up the warmth. There was a gentle breeze. It was exceptional weather for the end of January.

It was getting close to noon, and time for her little half, the Risperidal. I asked her if she would like some peaches and wheeled her into the house.   I pureed some canned peaches. The first bite had the crushed up pill in it. It went down fine. But after just a few more spoonfuls, she started coughing.

I took her to the couch and laid her on her side, but she couldn't stop. I tried suctioning, but it seemed like I couldn't get enough out to help. I called the number for the hospice nurse. They were there in just a few minutes. I explained about giving her the peaches, just enough to get her pill down, and about trying to suction her. I thought it would help to watch them do it. Maybe I wasn't doing it right. I didn't want to gag her. They tried, but weren't doing anything different than I was doing and it wasn't helping. They brought in a soft flexible tube to attach to the suction hose. They said it could be inserted further down into her airways. I was willing to let them try. After a couple of minutes of trying to get the tube down her throat and Mama gagging, I could see she didn't like it. I knew it wouldn't be worth the trouble. I told them to stop.

I had read that even if you successfully suction the fluids from the air passages that it would just come back and the process would have to be repeated again and again. I didn't want her to have to go through that. I talked to the nurses about it and they confirmed it to be true. I held Mama while I told them, "Let's just try the hydrocodone. Maybe that will help." So they helped me get the dose measured out and showed me how to drop it inside her cheek so it wouldn't make her cough and so it would be absorbed quickly. She had stopped coughing while they were trying to suction her.

They told me it wasn't helping her any to feed her. That it

would just cause her to cough more. I just nodded. I tried to wrap my mind around that, *How? How can I not feed her?* It was time to let go.

After they left, we stood in front of the window waiting for Papa to come home. I wrapped her arms around my waist, laid my head on her shoulder and cried quietly, "Mama, hold me while you can."

A TEDDY BEAR, SOME SUNSHINE, AND A SMILE

When Papa came home, she was resting peacefully on the couch. As he passed Mama on the couch, he rustled through his shopping bags and plopped a red and white Valentine teddy bear on Mama's tummy. The heart read, "Only You." After Papa set down his bags in the kitchen he came back in to sit on the floor by Nanny. So he could pet her and talk to her. "That's for Papa's little sweetheart."

I told him all about our experience with the coughing, the suctioning, and the nurses. Jack called. She was coming down for the weekend. Susan and Marty were coming over too.

We decided to go out for some more sunshine. We were thankful for that at least. We put the afghan around her shoulders and helped her walk out on the porch. She stood by the porch rail, soaking up the rays watching the familiar movements of their neighborhood.

A little later in the day, Arvilla came over from across the street to visit. It had been a month since she caught us out walking in front of her house and spoke to us. Arvilla wasn't out much these days, except to go the doctor. She sat there by Mama on the couch and we talked about what a beautiful day it was and we talked about heaven. We speculated if we love our lives and this world with all the pain and problems we go through, how much more we would love heaven. As Arvilla got up to leave, she looked back at Mama. My mother, ever the gracious host, gave her the last smile.

LAYING HER DOWN

After Jack got there, Mama started having trouble breathing again. We tried every position we could think of. We kept the oxygen on her, but it wasn't enough. Finally, we stood her up and it was easier for her to breathe. She was getting weaker and wasn't standing up straight so Jack and I stood on either side of her and held her up. We stood there a long time in front of the window while Jackie watched from his chair. We sang to her. Jack would sing a song, and then I would sing one. Mostly we hummed. We were trying to soothe her, to calm her, hoping to ease her struggles. We gave her the hydrocodone again when it was time and it helped to relax her.

Soon, Susan and Marty were there and it was time to move to the bedroom. I took her to the bathroom one last time and supported her as I led her to the bed. She sat down on the edge, but didn't want to lie down. She was fighting to breathe and couldn't sit up straight. Jack was on the

191

floor in front of her, Susan and Marty on either side. I brought a damp washcloth to wipe her face. We visited as we sat with her until she was so tired she *had* to lie down. The medicine would help her for awhile and she would rest quietly, but when it started wearing off, she would begin to moan.

Later, we called for the nurse again. He called in a prescription for something to help her not worry about anything, and something to help dry up some of the fluids in her airways. Soon he was back with the medicine that would ease her struggles. He explained how often we could give each one and how much we could give. He said we should try every two hours and if it wasn't enough, we could try giving it every hour and a half until we found what worked for us. We didn't want to give her too much, just enough to give her some relief. We got a notebook and pen and started keeping a log. I gave her the pain medicine and Jack gave her the two new ones.

It was late when Susan and Marty left for the night. I lay down on the couch thinking I might sleep for an hour or so. Jack was going to lie down with Mama for awhile. The house was quiet and dark except for the dim light from Mama's room. I could hear Mama moaning a little, and Jack humming. I knew she was lying beside Mama, stroking her hair, arranging her hands, and keeping her as comfortable as possible. Then Mama began to cry. My heart ached as I listened. Jack kept humming and held her while she cried her heart out. Mama was letting go of everything she loved in this world. She was saying good-bye.

ONE MORE DAY

We had to give her the medicine every hour to keep her from moaning. The nurse came back to check on us around midnight and checked her blood pressure. It wouldn't register the bottom number. The systolic or top number was only 75.

Somehow we all slept for a few hours early in the morning. We woke around six o'clock in the morning and realized we had missed two doses of medicine. She was starting to moan a little and her eyes flickered a little. We knew that family would be visiting so we got everything together to get her cleaned up. We didn't know if she would bounce back a little or not. We didn't think so.

Pajamas were too hard to get on and off, so we got her purple gown with the butterflies on it and cut it down the back to make it easier to put on. Jack and I gave her a quick bed bath – the only one she got. Then we put on the purple gown and her soft lavender sockies. We put a little pillow between her knees to keep her comfortable, brushed her hair and rolled her to her other side.

We had started giving the medicine every hour again, but it was almost eleven o'clock before she was resting quietly again.

It was another beautiful, warm, sunny day. I opened the blinds and let the sun stream in. As it warmed up, I opened the window so the fresh air could fill the room. I knelt down on the pillow that was on the floor at the head of her bed and talked to her. "How are you doing sweetheart? Let's go for another walk in the park, just you and me and the ducks."

I imagined a blink as I stroked her hair.

"The sun is shining, and it's warm outside and there are sparkles on the water today. Let's sit on our bench and look out across the water. Isn't it beautiful against the blue, blue sky?"

And even though her eyes were closed I saw them move, another blink.

THE GATHERING

There was a gathering of friends and family that day. The neighbors were concerned. The young couple that lives across the street wandered over to ask how Mama was doing. When Jackie told them what was going on with Mama, they took a minute to pray with him. There was so much food. In addition to the food everyone else was bringing, Mama's sister-in-law, Brenda, brought trays of sandwiches, with sides, and dessert from her restaurant. I was there when Brenda, leaned over and whispered to Mama, "Glenda, this is Brenda. Honey, we're sorry you are going through this. Everybody loves you."

The grandkids, most of them married and in their twenties now, looked at the picture albums Mama had put together and reminisced. One or two at a time, they would come to Mama's room and spend a few minutes or half an hour. We talked about what was new in our lives and reminded each other of the good times we've had. And each one knelt on that pillow or leaned over the bed to give Nanny a kiss before they had to go. Her hands and face were covered with kisses and tears.

As it got closer to bedtime, Susan and Bill's preacher came by. Jackie had asked him if he would perform the funeral service and he agreed. We gathered in the bedroom and listened as he read the 23rd Psalm. Then he prayed for us. It was a comfort to know others were praying for us.

SLIPPING AWAY

Bill and Susan reluctantly said their good nights, reminding us to call if anything happened. Marty had to go home and take care of her boys. We settled in for another night. We continued to give her the medicine every hour and she didn't wake up, she didn't moan, but her breathing became more labored as the night went on. We checked her to see if she needed a new pad every few hours, but there was nothing. Her body was shutting down.

As morning neared, her hands and arms became less rigid. All the tension was gone. There was no more tremor, no shaking. She was relaxed. We had not moved her during the night. She had lain mostly on her back but leaning to her right toward the center of the bed. Jack and I talked to Papa about moving her to her left side. It was a little after four o'clock. Since we were going to disturb her, we decided to take the opportunity to wash her face and hands with a warm washcloth. Then we straightened the bed and gently rolled her to her back and leaned her a little to her left side. Papa watched while Jack brushed her hair and I put lotion on her feet. The scent of Butterfly Flowers filled the room and I quietly sang her song.

It was my turn to hold her. I snuggled in next to her, tucking my knees behind hers, one hand propped under my head and the other hand holding hers. Her breathing was shallow now, no longer labored, almost a whisper. Papa was gathering his things for a shower. "I'm gonna get my shower before people start coming," he said.

Jack knelt down on the pillow beside the bed and stroked Nanny's hair. I was watching Nanny breathe. She hesitated for a second. "It's happening!" I whispered. "Jack, tell Papa to come quick, she's leaving us."

She stood and tried to get her dad's attention. "Dad come here."

"No, I won't be long," he said.

Jack went to the bedroom door. "It's time," she told him.

Then he understood and knelt down by Nanny and held her. Jack came around behind me and lay across the pillows above me and Mama.

I think she waited, so delicately balanced between two worlds, for Papa to get to her side, to take those last two short breaths and then she just slipped away silently and peacefully "She's gone now," I said softly. The room was so quiet and still for a moment. We knew it, but we couldn't believe it. The tears began to roll.

As we patted and rubbed each other's arms, Jack prayed, "Thank you Lord for taking her. You hold her now, like we've been holding her. Take her to Braxton. He needs her now."

A LAST GLIMPSE

We waited until Susan and Bill and Marty could get there before we called hospice. Hospice would call the coroner and would take care of everything else.

While Susan stood by Mama's bed, I gave her a big hug and just held her. I felt an assurance that we would become even closer as time goes on. There were so many things to talk about. So many things we could do together. Maybe the time we would have spent with Mama would now be spent with each other.

We still held our vigil in Mama's room. We were still trying to take care of her. We didn't want to leave her alone. We would only have her a little while longer. Marty sat on the pillow in the floor while I told her how we had held Mama while she passed. I told her how peaceful she was when she slipped away and about Jack's prayer. It was then that she told me how she made a decision to be faithful and live her life for Jesus the night that Braxton passed away.

Jackie's brother, Charlie, and his wife, Phyllis, arrived soon. And his brother Jerry was there. Arvilla's husband, David, came from across the street, to express his condolences. Jackie was surrounded by his brothers and sisters and I hoped they would continue to be there for him for awhile. I would need some time for myself soon. We had hardly slept at all the last two nights.

197

When the coroner got there, Jack and I went back to Mama's room for one last good-bye. I reached down to uncover and kiss her hands. But there was a note tucked between them. It made me cry to think of Jack sending her heartfelt words off with Mama on her last journey. "I can't read this," I said.

Jack said, "No, you can read it. It's okay."

And I said, "No, I can't read it because I can't see right now. You'll have to tell me later what you wrote."

They carried her gently from the bedroom to the stretcher in the living room. She was covered except for her beautiful legs with the lavender sockies. Her knees were still bent, her hands folded on her tummy holding her note, with the fragrance of butterflies, sunshine, flowers, and prayers. I wondered if the people at the funeral home would know how much she was loved.

Words of Hope

For Eternity

AFTERWARD

As we straightened the house and picked through the pictures, Marty came in with the triplets.

"Where's Nanny?" they asked.

Marty looked over the refrigerator door and apologetically said, "I've been over this with them."

"It's okay," I said. "I'm glad they asked." I turned to the boys, "She's in heaven with Jesus and Braxton. It's going to be a long, long time before we see her again."

Over the next few days, I would imagine her in the throne room in the presence of the Lord. I would see myself standing there with her and smile feeling the warmth of hope. In the weeks ahead, I would be amazed how much comfort and peace could be found by simply speaking the name of Jesus.

Jackie ironed Mama's favorite lime green monkey pajamas and hung them neatly on a hanger by the front door. I hugged the soft cloth close to me in the back of Marty's Suburban on the way to the funeral home. My throat ached as I gave up the pajamas to the young woman that greeted us. She looked curiously at the pajamas as I handed them to her and I had to smile.

OUR GIFT

We did it. We took care of her and we kept her as

201

comfortable as we could. We made it through the pads, the trips to the bathroom, and the bed changing. We made it through the pacing and the crying, the falling, the swallowing and eating problems, and we made it through the hard part at the end. We made the most of every day. And at the end she was at home, in her own bed, surrounded by those she loved. That was our gift to her.

JACK'S NOTE TO MAMA

When you and Dad came to pick me up that first time, I had already made up my mind that I wouldn't like you. I didn't want to share my daddy with you and I was going to do everything in my power to make things difficult for you. But from the moment I got in the car, something was different.

I remember one day telling you in anger, "You aren't my mother and I don't have to listen to you."

You just sat down beside me on the bed and said, "No, I'm not your mother, but you will listen to me. I will be to you whatever you will let me be. I love you, just like I love my girls. And I consider you to be one of my girls. I will do for you anything I would do for Susan and Pam."

After that, I told you how sorry I was and we became friends.

Later, as I raised my kids, our weekly calls were a source of strength and laughter. You taught me so much about love. My life would have been so different without you. I don't know what we're going to do without you. I love you.

Jack

MY NOTE TO YOU – THE READER

At some point in our lives, we become aware of the existence of God, the creator of the universe, and are given the opportunity to decide whether to seek, serve, and trust or to turn away. Many of us have turned away from His offer of love, not wanting to share our lives with Him, not trusting His guidance.

As we pass through this life, many of us may become angry at God for allowing so much suffering and pain and we may choose to use this as an excuse to ignore Him.

But if He could sit down beside you on the bed and have a talk, He might say, "I love you - just like I love my son, Jesus. In fact, if you will just give me your heart, I will consider you to be one of my children. I want to give you everything."

How can we resist His offer of love? Turn to Him. He will be a friend like no other.

He will walk with you through all the stages of your life. He will teach you how to love. Life would be so different without Him, but you don't have to worry about that. The Bible says, He will never leave you.

> *Have I not commanded you? Be strong and of good courage; do not be afraid, nor be dismayed, for the Lord your God is with you wherever you go.*
>
> *Joshua 1:7*

I am so thankful to God for the Bible. It is truly a treasure. Through the Word of God, we can know Him better. It is a source of comfort, strength, and direction.

It is the prayer of my heart that you would desire to know God better and have faith to trust Him completely. Remember, God looks at the heart. Pray earnestly and pray honestly. Seek the Lord and you will find Him.

Her Funeral

WORDS FROM THE FAMILY
(SPOKEN AT HER FUNERAL)

Mama. She was beautiful, elegant, and classy, but always modest and favoring the lasting styles. All the granddaughters enjoyed dressing up in Nanny's hat collection from time to time. She was truly a homemaker, for she made her home a wonderful place to be. She loved to sew and was an unforgettable cook. Holiday gatherings at Papa's and Nanny's were the best. Who could forget her apple pies, pumpkin rolls, and cheesecakes? Mmmm. She taught us manners and how to set the table and that families should eat together at the table with the TV off. Her home was always open and all of us kids enjoyed extended stays from time to time - some more than others. She was always welcoming. Even on Friday before she lay down for the last time, she gave a half smile to a visiting neighbor.

We could depend on her to give the best advice - whether we asked for it or not. But that was because she loved us so much and wanted the best for us. She was so strong. Her standards were high and she expected us to follow those standards as well. Of course we disappointed her at times, but she loved unconditionally, and never lost faith in any of us. She was full of goodness and grace. She was proud of her family and she prayed for her family. It was her greatest hope that she would see us all again. Mama, set a place for us.

If she could be here today, she might sing an old hymn that was dear to her heart. Here's the last verse:

Let us then be true and faithful
Trusting, serving every day

207

BLUE, BLUE SKY

Just one glimpse of Him in glory
Will the toils of life repay

When we all get to heaven
what a day of rejoicing that will be!
When we all see Jesus
we will sing and shout the victory!

SWEET BEULAH LAND

I'm kind of homesick for a country
To which I've never been before
No sad good-byes will there be spoken
For time won't matter any more

Beulah Land, I'm longing for you
And someday on thee I'll stand
There my home shall be eternal
Beulah Land, sweet Beulah Land

 I'm looking now across that river
Where my faith will end in sight
I've just a few more days to labor
Then I will take my heavenly flight

Beulah Land, I'm longing for you
And someday on thee I'll stand
 There my home shall be eternal
Beulah Land, sweet Beulah land

COME SPRING

I stood in the lonely room
of a mother old and grey,
Her voice so weak she could hardly speak.
I brushed a tear away.
She was watching the little snowflakes,
falling on her window pane.
She breathed a sigh and then replied,

"I'll be gone to be with Jesus come spring."

Before the roses bloom in my garden
 I'll be gathering flowers in a better land.
Before the fields are green, before the robin sings,
I'll be gone to be with Jesus come spring.

There's a big gate standing open.
A gentle voice calls me home.
Soon I'll be in God's country
in a garden all my own.
And with my troubles far behind me
and my body free from pain,
When the sun melts the snow
and the warm winds blow

 I'll be gone to be with Jesus come spring.

And now the roses bloom in her garden
And she's gathering flowers in a better land.
She's gone where angels sing.
Earth's loss is heaven's gain.
And we'll meet when God gathers flowers come spring.

I know we'll meet when God gathers flowers come spring.

SCRIPTURE AND PRAYER FROM THE CEMETERY SERVICE

I CORINTHIANS 15:35-58 (TLB)

But someone may ask, "How will the dead be brought back to life again? What kind of bodies will they have?" What a foolish question! You will find the answer in your own garden! When you put a seed into the ground it doesn't grow into a plant unless it "dies" first. And when the green shoot comes up out of the seed, it is very different from the seed you first planted. For all you put into the ground is a dry little seed of wheat, or whatever it is you are planting, then God gives it a beautiful new body - just the kind he wants it to have; a different kind of plant grows from each kind of seed. And just as there are different kinds of seeds and plants, so also there are different kinds of flesh. Humans, animals, fish, and birds are all different.

The angels in heaven have bodies far different from ours, and the beauty and the glory of their bodies is different from the beauty and the glory of ours. The sun has one kind of glory while the moon and stars have another kind. And the stars differ from each other in their beauty and brightness.

In the same way, our earthly bodies which die and decay are different from the bodies we shall have when we come back to life again, for they will never die. The bodies we have now embarrass us for they become sick and die; but they will be full of glory when we come back to life again. Yes, they are weak, dying bodies now, but when we live again they will be full of strength. They are just human bodies at death, but when they come back to life they will be superhuman bodies. For just as there are natural, human bodies, there are also supernatural, spiritual bodies.

The Scriptures tell us that the first man, Adam, was given a natural, human body but Christ is more than that, for he was life-giving Spirit.

First, then, we have these human bodies and later on God gives us spiritual, heavenly bodies. Adam was made from the dust of the earth, but Christ came from heaven above. Every human being has a body just like Adam's made of dust, but all who become Christ's will have the same kind of body as his - a body from heaven. Just as each of us now has a body like Adam's so we shall some day have a body like Christ's.

I tell you this, my brothers: an earthly body made of flesh and blood cannot get into God's kingdom. These perishable bodies of ours are not the right kind to live forever. But I am telling you this strange and wonderful secret: we shall not all die, but we shall all be given new bodies! It will all happen in a moment, in the twinkling of an eye, when the last trumpet is blown. For there will be a trumpet blast from the sky and all the Christians who have died will suddenly become alive, with new bodies that will never, never die; and then we who are still alive shall suddenly have new bodies too. For our earthly bodies, the ones we have now that can die, must be transformed into heavenly bodies that cannot perish but will live forever.

When this happens, then at last this Scripture will come true – "Death is swallowed up in victory." O death, where then your victory? Where then your sting? For sin – the sting that causes death – will all be gone; and the law, which reveals our sins, will no longer be our judge. How we thank God for all of this! It is he who makes us victorious through Jesus Christ our Lord!

So, my dear brothers, since future victory is sure, be strong and steady, always abounding in the Lord's work, for you know that nothing you do for the Lord is ever wasted as it would be if there were no resurrection.

PHILIPPIANS 4:4-9 (TLB)

Always be full of joy in the Lord; I say it again, rejoice! Let everyone see that you are unselfish and considerate in all you do. Remember that the Lord is coming soon. Don't worry about anything; instead, pray about everything; tell God your needs and don't forget to thank him for his answers. If you do this you will experience God's peace,

which is far more wonderful than the human mind can understand.
His peace will keep your thoughts and your hearts quiet and at rest
as you trust in Christ Jesus.
And now brothers, as I close this letter let me say this one more thing:
Fix your thoughts on what is true and good and right. Think about
things that are pure and lovely, and dwell on the fine. good things in
others. Think about all you can praise God for and be glad about.
Keep putting into practice all you learned from me and saw me doing,
and the God of peace will be with you.

Father,
We thank you for this day,
For the dusk and the dawn,
The changing seasons,
And the beauty of the earth.
Thank you for Mama,
For who she was,
And for the joy she brought to this family.
She was such a wonderful blessing to us all.
We miss her so much.

Lord,
We don't understand
Why she suffered
In this life.
But we are confident
And thankful
That she is with You
And that she is whole again.
 I ask that you would comfort
Our friends and our family and
That the peace that passes understanding
Would keep our hearts and minds
And that each of us would be found ready
At Your return.

Some Pictures

Mama was born in 1943. She was the youngest in this picture. One more brother came later.

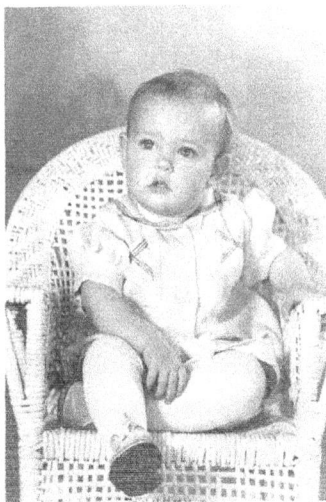

This picture of Mom as a toddler sits on Jackie's bedside table.

Mama as a teenager with her mother

Mama and Daddy on their honeymoon.
I was just a baby when they met.

Mama, Susan, and me in Oklahoma City
They wrapped me up like a mummy
so I could hand out candy.

Mama and Jackie married in 1974

The table set for Christmas dinner

1986 The best of times

Mother's Day 2008

Getting some sunshine by the garden
Early Spring 2010

Eating peanut butter and jelly - Summer 2010

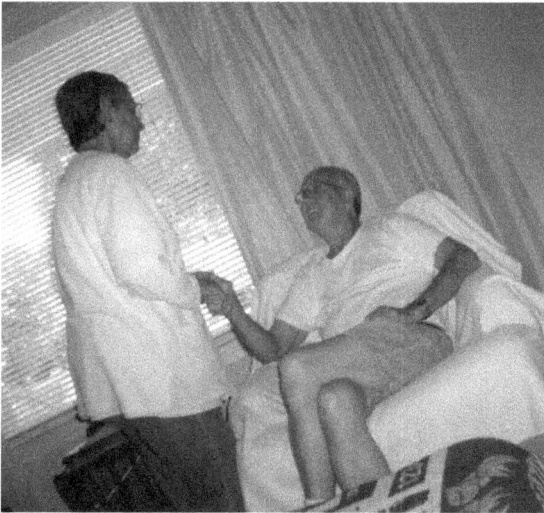

Papa holding her hands to keep them from shaking and
telling her the things that make her smile.

Sitting on the back porch with that far away look
Late Summer 2010

All prettied up playing her piano - Autumn 2010

Sunset - Autumn 2013